'This is the book that students, lecturers, trainers and mentors have been calling for to enable anti-racist good practice in teacher education. Rooted in expert knowledge and based on the outcomes of a fascinating research project giving voice to staff and students involved in an inner-city PGCE course, it provides real-life examples of good practice and the hidden barriers identified by students and tutors themselves. The authors strike an excellent balance between recognising the pressures on teacher educators while highlighting the desperate need for safe institutional spaces for curriculum development and to reassess the everyday behaviours and attitudes that perpetuate racism. For too long research has shown us that race policies do not always filter through to practices and the ground. This valuable, clearly written and timely book covering conceptual understanding, recruitment, retention, curriculum development, reflective practice and tools for making changes is a vital contribution to teacher education.'

Julie Hall, Co-chair Staff and Educational Development Association (SEDA) and Director of Learning and Teaching Enhancement, University of Roehampton

'This book provides a straightforward and pragmatic approach to dealing with issues that are all too often fraught with feeling. The helpful approach of a narrative with examples organised thematically provides for readers who want to just dip in as well as for more thoroughgoing consideration. Recommended.'

David Ruebain, Chief Executive, Equality Challenge Unit

'In an increasingly diverse world where notions of difference are no longer regarded as stable or fixed, Mirza and Meetoo help readers to see the complexity of difference. The challenge of globalization is to see the full humanity of every person—to recognize that each is more than the sum total of his or her race, class, gender, language, national origin, faith, sexual identity, or ability. As human beings we organize ourselves in infinite combinations that are special, indeed sacred to us all, and until we truly respect difference we will not understand democracy. *Respecting Difference* is a great start.'

Professor Gloria Ladson-Billings, Kellner Family Chair in Urban Education and Professor of Curriculum and Instruction and Educational Policy Studies, University of Wisconsin-Madison

RESPECTING DIFFERENCE

RESPECTING DIFFERENCE

RACE, FAITH AND CULTURE FOR TEACHER EDUCATORS

HEIDI SAFIA MIRZA AND VEENA MEETOO

Institute of Education, University of London
Issues in Practice

Leading education
and social research
Institute of Education
University of London

First published in 2012 by the Institute of Education,
University of London, 20 Bedford Way, London WC1H 0AL

www.ioe.ac.uk/publications

British Library Cataloguing in Publication Data:

A catalogue record for this publication is available from the
British Library

ISBN 978 0 85473 887 8

Typeset by Quadrant Infotech (India) Pvt Ltd

Printed and bound by CPI Group (UK) Ltd, Croydon, CR0 4YY

Contents

List of Abbreviations

BME	Black and minority ethnic
BT	Beginning teacher
CRT	Critical race theory
DFE	Department for Education
EBITT	Employment-based initial teacher training
EHRC	Equality and Human Rights Commission
ECU	Equality Challenge Unit
GEO	Government Equalities Office
GLA	Greater London Authority
HEI	Higher Education Institute
ITE	Initial teacher education
ITT	Initial teacher training
NQT	Newly qualified teachers
NUT	The National Union of Teachers
NASUWT	National Association of Schoolmasters/Union of Women Teachers
OTTP	Overseas Trained Teacher Programme
PGCE	Post Graduate Certificate in Education
QTS	Qualifying to teach standards
SCITT	School-centred initial teacher training
TDA	The Training and Development Agency for Schools

ACKNOWLEDGEMENTS

We would like to thank the participants in this study who generously shared their experiences of race, faith and culture and their visions of good practice. Their honesty and professional commitment made this publication possible. A special acknowledgement must go to Gregg Beratan, the consultant researcher on phase one of the project whose knowledge of inclusive education shaped our direction. Thank you to the project advisory team whose expertise and rigour kept us on track, in particular Ruth Carter, Anton Franks, Andy Ash, Christine Callender, Vini Lander and Nova Matthias. There have been many others involved in creating the vision for this book. We would like to mention especially the IOE Publications team: Jim Collins, Jonathan Dore and Sally Sigmund. Finally thank you to the Training and Development Agency for Schools (TDA) who funded this research through their innovative Recruitment and Retention Challenge Grant (RRCG).

Every effort has been made to trace copyright holders and to obtain their permission for the use of copyrighted material. The publisher apologises for any errors or omissions and would be grateful for notification of any corrections that should be incorporated in future reprints or editions of this book.

ABOUT THE AUTHORS

Heidi Safia Mirza is Professor of Equalities Studies in Education at the Institute of Education, University of London, UK. She has published extensively on the intersectionality of gender and race, including studies on ethnicity and educational attainment, multiculturalism and the experiences of Muslim and minority ethnic women. Her research includes the European Union project *Young Migrant Women in Secondary Education*. She has held a number of senior public appointments including the Schools Standards Task Force where she shaped many initiatives for raising equality standards in education for black and minority ethnic students. She is author of several best-selling books including *Young, Female and Black* and *Race, Gender and Educational Desire: Why Black Women Succeed and Fail*.

Veena Meetoo is Research Officer at the Thomas Coram Research Unit, Institute of Education, University of London. She has conducted research into social justice and inequalities, particularly the intersections of gender, race, ethnicity and migration. Her current research focuses on young minority ethnic women in secondary education, and addresses issues including gender-based violence, bullying and processes of racialisation. Veena has co-authored several publications including *Tackling the Roots of Racism* (with Bhavnani and Mirza, 2005), *Young, Female and Migrant: Gender, Class and Racial Identity in Multicultural Britain* (with Mirza, 2011).

CHAPTER 1
A STUDY IN RACE, FAITH AND CULTURE

INTRODUCTION

One thing became clear when listening to tutors.
There is no singular 'best practice' – just lots of 'good practices'.

Black and minority ethnic students are valued members of our learning and teaching community. Their diverse and different outlooks enrich the learning culture and experience of all students and staff on our programmes and courses. But do white tutors, trainers, lecturers and mentors working with black and minority ethnic students understand the nature of their specific learning and life experiences? Do they as professional teacher educators have the teaching practice skills and knowledge to deal with issues as they arise for black and minority ethnic students on their courses? Addressing these questions from a practical perspective is at the heart of this book.

The aim of this book is to identify and share good practice that tutors and lecturers have developed when engaging with black and minority ethnic students. It addresses the issues as raised by the students and the tutors themselves. It provides short, clear and accessible guidance based on evidence from the tutors' own practice and students' experience. The objective of this book is to bring hidden issues that could be seen as having a racial origin out into the open to be dealt with fairly and professionally.

THE STUDY

This study offers a small-scale snapshot of policy and practice on the Post Graduate Certificate in Education (PGCE) and is therefore by no means conclusive in its findings. The research was carried out between 2007 and 2008 in a higher education institution (HEI) that provides initial teacher training (ITT).[1] The HEI was situated in a large multicultural city in England, and though the student body was ethnically diverse – 27 per cent of all students were black and minority ethnic – all the tutors we interviewed, except one, were white. The first phase of the project consisted of 14 face-to-face interviews with male and female tutors from the primary, secondary and post-compulsory branches of the PGCE. An outcome of phase one was a best practice booklet that we developed from the findings. The booklet was disseminated to all the tutors on the PGCE. The second phase was a follow-up and consisted of a grounded evaluation of the good practice guidance developed from phase one. To achieve this we consulted widely, holding three focus groups with a total of 23 primary, secondary and post-compulsory PGCE tutors. We also conducted four in-depth semi-structured interviews

1

with secondary and post-compulsory tutors and received 20 written feedback evaluations on the guidance from tutors. In phase two, we also held one focus group with 15 black, minority ethnic and white secondary male and female beginning teachers (BTs) to gain a student perspective. It was vital to understand their experiences on the PGCE. Student experiences were fundamental for framing the study's findings, particularly in respect of racist incidents and the dynamics of institutional racism.

The case studies in this book are intended to highlight some of the specific ways in which tutors approached issues of visible race, faith and cultural difference when supporting black and minority ethnic students throughout the PGCE course. To ensure complete confidentiality, our findings are written up as anonymous composite case studies.[2] The cases are drawn from representative accounts reflecting real professional experiences. It is important to note that while each case is complex and located in specific circumstances, they do not represent any single tutor or student or event. Names of the tutors as well as courses have been changed to maintain anonymity. The interviews are also anonymised in the same way, but are still direct quotations from the tutors and students who participated in the research.

In the research, the tutors openly engaged with the process of data collection and shared their experiences and practices. They described what they see as crucial issues for black and minority ethnic students. From their experience of the recruitment and retention of black and minority ethnic students, there appeared to be a link between tackling issues of racism, respecting cultural and faith-based knowledge, and the student's well-being and ability to progress and stay the course.

One thing became clear when listening to tutors – there is no singular 'best practice', just lots of 'good practices'. This book is an attempt to gather together some of those good practices so that professionals can use the material as a resource to develop their ongoing reflective, questioning and critical perspectives on issues to do with racism and the educational well-being of black and minority ethnic students.

It is hoped this book will open a dialogue about tackling issues of racism at a personal and professional level and so enable us to support our black and minority ethnic students through their programmes of learning, enabling them to become much needed and valued future teachers and educational leaders.

WHY FOCUS ON RACE, FAITH AND CULTURE?

There is no single racism, but multiple racisms; colour racism must be examined together with cultural racism, which includes ethnicity, religion and language.

(Fredman, 2001: 2)

In this book we collectively use race, faith, and culture as a concept that frames the everyday way we talk about racial and ethnic difference. As the census categories show, there is no one rationale that underpins our thinking about race, faith and culture (Platt, 2011). Sometimes official surveys use visible skin colour (like 'black'), sometimes citizenship or place of birth (like Pakistan). At other times culture, language, religion, region or country is used to identify and categorise our racial and ethnic origins.

We recognise the heightened and sensitive nature of using 'racial' terms and categories, but also acknowledge there is no consistent or single way to do it. For example the government has adopted as their official term 'black and minority ethnic', shortened to BME in many of their reports. This is not a term many 'minority ethnic' communities tend to use to describe themselves. Indeed there has been much controversy about what it really signifies and to whom. For example, the label 'ethnic minority' ironically refers to peoples who make up majority populations globally, such as Asians or Africans, who yet find themselves defined as 'minority' migrant communities in the UK. In response to this, some choose more empowering terms and refer to themselves as 'minority ethnic' or as 'global majority populations' in the UK.

DEFINING 'RACE' AND ETHNICITY

Here in this book we still use the official and much contested collective term 'black and minority ethnic' (BME). While it denotes the social construction of difference through visible 'race' (black) and cultural (ethnic) markers, it does not however acknowledge that racism is increasingly being framed in terms of visible faith-based difference since the (Muslim) terrorist attacks of 9/11. Hence in the book we also refer to 'visible race, faith and cultural difference' as many tutors' accounts of racism were framed in terms of visible religious cultural ethnic groups. However it must be recognised that the category 'black and minority ethnic teachers' is itself very diverse, comprising different nationalities and cultural backgrounds. Policies and strategies for black and minority ethnic teachers and students must take account of this diversity.

The different ways in which racial terms evolve help us understand the political and historical evolution of racial definitions (Bhavnani *et al.*, 2005). It is now generally accepted that there is no scientific or biological foundation for racial difference. Thus 'race' is deemed a social construct (hence the quotation marks). When people use the term 'black' to self-identify, it is understood not to constitute a real or fixed (essential) 'race' category. Instead, it is a politically contested umbrella term that has come to mean post-colonial peoples who are visibly and politically positioned as racialised 'others' (Mirza, 1997).

The changing manifestations of racisms reflect ideological attempts to legitimate domination in different social and historical contexts. 'Race' is therefore not about objective measurable physical and social characteristics, but about relationships of domination and subordination. Racism is expressed in different ways in particular historical times and within regional and national contexts. In other words, there are different racisms at any one time (see Key Point Summary 1.1).

KEY POINT SUMMARY 1.1: MULTIPLE RACISMS

According to Fredman (2001: 2), 'There is no single racism, but multiple racisms; colour racism must be examined together with cultural racism, which includes ethnicity, religion and language'. Racism, in Fredman's schema, operates along at least three axes:

- First, it is characterised by denigratory stereotyping, hatred and violence.
- Second, it sets in motion cycles of disadvantage.
- Third it negates and even obliterates the culture, religion and language of the groups concerned.

Educational interventions therefore need to be cognisant of all three axes of racism if they are to have an impact.

One way to tackle the deep roots of racism in our societies is to understand the ways in which we think and talk about racism in everyday contexts and the tiny inequities that are perpetuated through everyday practices. It is the micro everyday behaviours and attitudes that maintain the macro social structures of racism. The unwitting process whereby thoughtless, everyday discriminatory practices become an ingrained part of the ethos or culture of an organisation has been referred to as institutional racism. This is tackled in more detail in Chapter 5.

WHY FOCUS ON BLACK AND MINORITY ETHNIC TEACHERS?

Black and minority ethnic teachers bring diverse and different outlooks that enrich the learning cultures in our schools. With a quarter of all primary and secondary pupils in Britain now coming from minority ethnic backgrounds[3] it is essential to have educational systems that reflect the British population, and accept and value the differences that minority ethnic groups bring.

The issue of under-representation in the teaching profession and the consequent impact on the achievement of black and minority ethnic pupils was raised as long ago as 1985 in the Swann Report. Despite four decades marked by progressive equality legislation to positively promote race and gender equality and for people with disabilities, the case for an inclusive teaching profession still remains compelling (see Key Point Summary 1.2).

KEY POINT SUMMARY 1.2: WHY EMPLOY BME TEACHERS?

The following moral and 'business case' reasons for having more black and minority ethnic teachers have been put forward:[5]

- Everyone should receive fair treatment and equal opportunity to teach.
- Black and minority ethnic teachers can act as role models for black and minority ethnic students as well as counter stereotypes about ethnic minorities.
- Black and minority ethnic teachers may have a better understanding of local communities and pupils with similar cultural backgrounds. They may also serve an educative role for white students.
- Minority staff can reassure minority people who may not trust others. Black and minority ethnic parents may be more willing to communicate with them and so have their voices heard within schools.
- It is desirable to have some relation between the local population and the composition of the teaching body in a school.
- The teaching profession will be enriched by embracing the full diversity of experiences found in the wider society.

Black and minority ethnic teachers still only make up 6.3 per cent of the teacher workforce.[4] The highest proportion of black and minority ethnic teachers can be found in London in the boroughs of Hackney, Lambeth and Southwark (16 to 18 per cent). In contrast almost 50 per cent of the pupil population in these boroughs are from black and minority ethnic communities (Black Teachers in London, 2006).

THE NUMBERS GAME

Recruitment and retention of black and minority ethnic trainees onto ITE programmes is a major challenge. They are considered to be an under-represented group, alongside people with disabilities and male primary teachers (Bielby *et al.*, 2007). Many organisations set targets to increase the numbers of black and minority ethnic employees as a way of achieving diversity in the workforce. However just 'getting them in' does not in itself challenge institutional racism and there are many personal and emotional costs of 'just being there' to those who are targeted (Mirza, 2009). On the other hand targets can challenge entrenched racist practices and provide equal opportunities through opening access. A strategy of the Training and Development Agency for Schools (TDA throughout, though now renamed the Teaching Agency) has been to focus on attracting more black and minority ethnic teachers into the profession. Some progress has been made with 12 per cent of new entrants to ITE coming from a black and minority ethnic background in 2005/6 (Adonis, 2008). However recruitment is just the tip of the iceberg. Retention of black and minority ethnic staff is a far more pressing issue. Among black and minority ethnic trainees, 24 per cent failed to achieve Qualified Teacher Status on their courses compared to just 12 per cent for white trainees (Adonis, 2008). This shortfall is deeply worrying as it has been estimated that at least 15 to 20 per cent of teacher training places need to be taken up by black and minority ethnic trainees in the next two decades if we are to have a teaching workforce that represents not only the local BME communities but also the national British community (Ross, 2003).

RACISM AND DISCRIMINATION IN THE TEACHER WORKFORCE

Research has identified continuing discrimination as a major factor preventing black and minority ethnic people from becoming teachers and remaining in the teaching profession:

- The survey *Leadership aspirations and careers of Black and minority ethnic teachers* found more than half the sample reported some form of discrimination. Discrimination on the grounds of race and ethnicity amounted to four times the proportion of discrimination reported in respect to gender, age or faith. This varied among ethnic groups. Three-quarters of African teachers (significantly more so for men than women) experienced ethnic discrimination compared to 20 per cent of Caribbean and Indian teachers. However discrimination on the grounds of faith was reported four times more frequently by Pakistani teachers (McNamara *et al.*, 2010).

- The survey *Teachers' Careers: The impact of age, disability, ethnicity, gender and sexual orientation* found black and Asian teachers were half as likely to be head teachers and deputy head teachers as white teachers. Black and minority ethnic teachers were most likely to go for promotion but least likely to get it. They were often qualified, but rarely found in positions that reflected their ability and skill. The teachers themselves felt they were subjectively assessed for promotion by governors and head teachers. These 'assessors' were perceived as holding implicitly racist opinions. The teachers were also more likely to leave the profession, entered the profession later, and had lower professional satisfaction levels (Powney *et al.*, 2003).

RACISM IN THE CLASSROOM

There is a history of black and minority ethnic teachers facing overt racism, especially in terms of racist comments from pupils and parents (Siraj-Blatchford, 1991). One in six newly qualified teachers in Carrington *et al.*'s (2001) survey experienced racial harassment in their first posts, primarily from children. A national study, *Show Racism the Red Card*, found 83 per cent of questionnaire respondents from across the teaching profession had witnessed racist behaviour amongst their pupils (SRtRC, 2011a). While many felt there were strong racist attitudes amongst their pupil cohort, they also reported intentional and unintentional racist behaviour amongst some teachers, which ranged from the use of racist terminology and jokes to teachers having lower expectations of pupils from black, Asian or other minority ethnic groups. Tackling such behaviour is not always seen as a priority for school managers (Cole and Stuart, 2005). More common are subtler forms of covert institutional racism, for instance, having decisions and one's ability challenged by pupils and teachers, and resentfulness towards black and minority ethnic leaders (Bush *et al.*, 2006).

KEY ISSUES FOR BUILDING CAPACITY

Much needs to be done to support the development of black and minority ethnic teachers. Some of the tensions and barriers to overcome are:

GLASS CEILINGS AND CAREER DEVELOPMENT

A range of factors are seen to inhibit the career development of black and minority ethnic teachers including lack of role models, experience of racism, poor prospects and lack of career advice (Bariso, 2001). As a result many black and minority ethnic people do not join the profession and of those who do, many do not adequately progress and are deprived of pay and status (Maylor *et al.*, 2003; Ross, 2003). Black Teachers in London (2006) notes that black and minority ethnic teachers are often given responsibilities for 'soft' areas such as equal opportunities where they are seen to have 'specialist' knowledge (Jones, Maguire and Watson, 1997; Pole, 2001) rather than the 'hard' areas relating to management, leadership and policy. Sometimes this results from an ability to communicate, linguistically and culturally with parents who depend on particular teachers as a conduit for communicating with the school. However, while black and minority ethnic teachers can be seen as 'cultural experts' and role models, this is rarely recognised in terms of career advancement (Pole, 1999; WRECC, 1999). Poor staff development and promotion are seen as major reasons for black teachers leaving the profession. Some black teachers mention a racial 'glass ceiling' and 'invisible' criteria of selection panels (Ross, 2003; Powney *et al.*, 2003; McNamara *et al.*, 2010). However, despite perceived low pay and status of teaching careers, many are highly motivated and committed to teaching.

ROLE MODELS AND THE BURDEN OF REPRESENTATION

Black and minority ethnic teachers are often portrayed, and indeed may portray themselves, as role models and experts on black communities. As Portelli and Campbell-Stephens (2009) explain, 'servant leadership' (without the servitude!) in African and Asian communities sees leadership grounded in moral purpose in challenging social situations as part of a 'calling' or 'vocation'. While this may be true in many cases, there is a danger of only viewing black and minority ethnic teachers through these lenses. Black and minority ethnic teachers may be motivated by becoming role models but they are much more than 'charismatic heroes' (Carrington and Skelton, 2003). Such a limiting view may also add to the stresses of placements and teaching. Furthermore, it is inappropriate for an institution to make such an assumption. Black and minority ethnic teachers also emphasise that sharing a similar background is not sufficient to gain respect – at times the opposite can be true as teachers can be accused of 'acting white' (Osler, 1997). Black and minority ethnic teachers and leaders are also wary of being seen as special cases. Leaders are likely to stress that their leadership skills transcend ethnicity issues and that all leaders have to contend with cultural/contextual problems of one kind or another (Bush *et al.*, 2006).

NETWORKING AND MENTORING FOR EMPOWERMENT

Black and minority ethnic student teachers and teachers, including head teachers and lecturers, are often isolated and marginalised from informal and formal professional networks. This has a strong impact on their well-being and career progression (Osler, 1997; Harris *et al.*, 2003; McNamara, 2010; Hey *et al.*, 2011). Black and minority ethnic mentoring networks, professional groups and programmes provide safe cultural spaces for identity validation and shared knowledge generation that enables black and minority ethnic groups collectively to redress processes of racist exclusion through building affirming and empowering relationships (Dingus, 2008). For example, the National Union of Teachers' (NUT) Black Members' group holds a vibrant annual conference; and the Investing in Diversity Programme (IiD) at the Institute of Education, University of London (IOE) develops culturally literate leadership in London schools (Portelli and Campbell-Stephens, 2009).

ENDNOTES

1. There are currently 240 providers of initial teacher education (ITE) or initial teacher training (ITT) in England and approximately 40,000 people enter to train as teachers; 19 per cent of the places are allocated to undergraduate programmes; 59 per cent to postgraduate programmes; 18 per cent for employment-based routes and 4 per cent for school-based routes in 2007–08. About 85 per cent of ITE places, (mostly PGCE places), are allocated to higher education institutions (HEIs) and the rest to other providers (House of Commons Select Committee Report, 2010). There are about 85 universities offering ITE programmes; 60 SCITT (school-centred initial teacher training) and 102 EBITT (employment-based training) provision across England some of which will overlap since some universities and SCITTs also offer employment-based training routes (www.tda.gov.uk).

2. Here we draw on a Critical Race Theory (CRT) methodology which advocates storytelling and the use of composite characters to conceal and protect the participants' identities (Gillborn, 2008; Solórzano and Yosso, 2002).

3. There were 26.5 per cent of pupils in state-funded primary schools classified as being of minority ethnic origin and 22.2 per cent of pupils in state-funded secondary schools (Department for Education, 2011a). In inner London, more than half of school pupils (54.1 per cent) are recorded as learning English as an additional language. In maintained primary schools 16 per cent of pupils' first language was known or believed to be other than English. In state-funded secondary schools 11.6 per cent of pupils' first language was known or believed to be other than English (DFE, 2010).

4. The vast majority of teachers in service are from white ethnic groups (93.7 per cent). Asian teachers made up the next largest group (3 per cent). Black African Caribbean teachers made up 1.9 per cent of those in service followed by mixed white/other, 0.8 per cent. The final 0.7 per cent of teachers in service came from other ethnic backgrounds (DFE, 2011b).

5. See Swann, 1985; Ghuman, 1995; Bariso, 2001; Bush *et al.*, 2006; McNamara *et al.*, 2010; SRtRC, 2011a.

CHAPTER 2

GETTING IN THE DOOR: FAIR ADMISSIONS AND RECRUITMENT PRACTICE

ADMISSIONS AND RECRUITMENT STRATEGIES

Fair and equal admissions and recruitment practices are vital to improving retention of black and minority ethnic students on the PGCE. They strengthen the quality of candidates as well as opening up new and diverse opportunities for our institutions to flourish. Our research found tutors used a range of strategies to develop recruitment of black and minority ethnic students to the PGCE. These included the following examples of good practice:

- **Targeted advertising**, which included, but was not limited to, advertising with black community-based newspapers such as *The Voice*, as well as in community organisation newsletters, bulletin boards and other outlets that are more directly connected to minority ethnic communities.

- **Strategic links with undergraduate programmes** in universities serving higher numbers of minority ethnic students. These links took a variety of forms, including speaking about the PGCE to students on courses that would logically feed into particular subject areas (i.e. Geography, English, Drama, Science etc.).

- **Pre-admissions workshops for students** designed and targeted to help black and minority ethnic students reflect on their skills and what they would bring to teaching and to assist them in making the best application possible. They helped students understand how to better sell themselves by explaining how to develop their personal statements, draft their applications and prepare for the interview process. The workshops needed to be well advertised and integrated into the recruitment culture of the course for them to be well attended.

- **Short-listing workshops for tutors** using anonymised applications to get tutors to examine the short-listing process. The applications were used to enable tutors not only to reflect on the criteria they used to accept or reject candidates, but also on what they saw as potential for success.

- **Flexible admissions policies** that value more than just the minimum degree award required for admission.[1] Many of the tutors suggested that it was vital that the HEI be flexible in what it values in PGCE applicants in terms of wider experience and qualifications. *Several tutors commented on their reluctance to take explicitly 'affirmative action' that might lead to the 'dilution* *of quality'*. A good clear admissions policy that is regularly revised by the course team is essential to maintain an ongoing assessment of how changing institutional entry requirements and subjective assumptions can impact on different categories of students with different initial qualifications.

CASE STUDY
KEITH: A CASE OF IMPROVING OPPORTUNITIES IN ADMISSIONS AND RECRUITMENT

Keith, a 22-year-old African Caribbean biology student from an undergraduate programme in a new university in south London, was advised by one of his tutors not to apply to the high status HEI where he wished to do his PGCE. He was told that African Caribbean students had difficulty getting in because of the minimum degree requirements. A tutor from the HEI came to speak to one of Keith's classes about the PGCE. During the session Keith mentioned the advice he had been given. The HEI tutor said that while standards were high, they were flexible and that they recognised that there was much more to being a good teacher than subject knowledge. He told Keith that because of the HEI's link with his university, there were a number of students from his university who had completed the PGCE, with whom he could speak. The HEI tutor put him in touch with another student who shared his experience with Keith and recommended that he apply. Keith then requested an application form from the HEI's Registry. In the pack he found a notice for a pre-admissions workshop to help candidates through the application and admissions process.

In the workshop Keith discussed his interests and experiences. The tutor told him what he should emphasise in his application and personal statement for it to stand out, and how to approach the interview process. He warned Keith that in an attempt to be honest and reflective, many students over-emphasise their weaknesses and under-emphasise their strengths. Keith submitted his application and was granted an interview. The interview brought out more than just Keith's academic history and enabled him to present a much broader picture of himself and the kind of teacher he would be. He was successful and was accepted on the course.

CASE STUDY
SAM: A CASE OF POSITIVE ACTION AND DIFFERENT ROUTES INTO TEACHING

Sam a 42-year-old black British African student applied to the primary PGCE. He had been educated in Nigeria and had been living for many years in Britain. He had a third-class degree in engineering from a new university, but he had not managed to get a good job since graduating. He ended up in a series of casual jobs for several years. He was now a volunteer youth and community worker on an after-school project on a large and troubled council estate. He enjoyed the challenges of teaching very much. He recently had two children and was committed to becoming a primary teacher in maths and science to help him explore their development and understand them better. Dave and Linda, the two white tutors on the interviewing panel disagreed about his admission to the course. Dave said it would be unfair to accept Sam since they couldn't give him the time and support he needed to bring him up to the level expected. He argued that though there was a national drive to recruit more men, especially black and minority ethnic men, into primary teaching, he believed positive action to support students can put them in a difficult situation as it is not a level playing field. Ultimately he argued against admitting Sam because even though he could make a good teacher, he did not think he would survive the course. Linda however stressed that the different routes that ethnic minority students come through enrich the course and the different understandings of education and culture that Sam would bring with him are just as important. Sam was finally admitted and completed the course. He did struggle with his assignments and he did experience some unfair treatment and discrimination in his placement. He needed extra tutor support to help him challenge and overcome the situation.

REFUGEES AND OVERSEAS-TRAINED TEACHERS

Tutors explained how overseas-trained teachers and refugees are at a disadvantage in the admissions and recruitment process. Unlike British-born black and minority ethnic students they had particular issues when it came to accessing courses:

- First, their qualifications are often not recognised in the UK. They are required to possess a degree that is equivalent to the UK system verified through NARIC (National Recognition Information Centre for the UK). This is a lengthy and difficult process and many do not get through this hurdle.

- Second, many experience difficulty in obtaining their papers and references from their home country, which hinders admission.

- Third, many had degrees in shortage subjects and were keen to qualify to teach in UK schools or were already teachers but they did not have the level of English language required to function as a qualified teacher. Tutors thought short intensive courses covering English for academic purposes as well as modern idiomatic usage would make a big difference.

- Fourth, many failed to get through the interview process and needed support on how to represent themselves in the best possible light. For example, many did not mention important details in their CVs in relation to qualifications or experience obtained in their home country, as they believed these are not valued in the UK.

- Fifth, many had no experience of UK schools and were badly in need of sound advice and guidance to help them navigate the confusing maze of teacher training routes and career pathways in schools.

CASE STUDY
AMINA: A GOOD CULTURAL AND LINGUISTIC 'FIT'

Amina, a Somali woman, had a degree in business studies and a range of qualifications from further education (FE) institutions in the UK, providing foundations for HE study. As part of a teaching access course for refugees, she was placed in a community primary school in north London serving a catchment area that is culturally and economically diverse. She reported having a rewarding 'shadowing' experience. The staff had been supportive and she had been allowed the flexibility to choose any class she wished. She was encouraged to ask questions, all of which were considered and answered. Before she finished she was asked to come back for a 'one-to-one' class with two Somali students who had arrived six months ago and could not speak English. The school thought one Somali girl was struggling because of language problems. Amina translated the tests into her mother-tongue language but the girl still couldn't do them, indicating that there were other learning issues. At the end of the placement, Amina was asked if she would like to work as a volunteer for two days per week, particularly with Somali students new to English. She accepted the offer with the view to asking for paid employment once established at the school. She eventually got a part-time job in the school and successfully applied to do the PGCE with support from the specialist refugee adviser.

CASE STUDY
MAJID: A CASE OF DISABILITY ACCESS AND THWARTED AMBITIONS

Majid was a qualified secondary school teacher from Iran with a first-class bachelor's degree in modern foreign languages. He had been working for a few years as a student support worker in a secondary school in Britain but needed a British teaching qualification. He applied to do the access course aimed at refugees who wished to train as teachers in UK schools. The course included a two-week work-shadowing placement in a school. However, finding a placement for Majid, who had mobility needs, proved particularly difficult. Approaches were made to 20 schools in his vicinity but wheelchair access was an issue, especially since the student's placement had to be in a Modern Foreign Languages Department, which for some reason tend to be located on the top floor of many schools! A school some distance from the student's residence was eventually identified, and taxi transport offered by the Disability Support Team, but the additional difficulties this presented the student in terms of time and preparation made it untenable. Majid came to realise that a school environment was probably not the best for him because of his health conditions, and he voluntarily withdrew from the course. With the support of a specialist refugee career adviser on the access project in the HEI, Majid explored alternative career choices and decided to pursue a master's degree programme at a prestigious college in the University of London. Majid's experience highlights the barrier of access for disabled people seeking a career in teaching.

WHAT THE RESEARCH SAYS

STUDENT CHOICE

Black and minority ethnic student choice of HEIs does not follow the market-driven ideology. Unlike their white counterparts, these students' choices are moulded by a sense of who they are and their place in relation to race, class and gender. Families have a greater influence over black and minority ethnic student decisions. This is particularly true for young Muslim Pakistani and Bangladeshi women (**Housee**, 2004).

The learner identities of black and minority working-class students are reflected in their university 'choice' (**Reay** *et al.*, 2005). They tend to stick to what they know is achievable and comfortable and stay close to home. They often know people such as family members or friends within the newer universities and commented that they seemed like friendlier places. PGCE students commented on how their familiarity with the HEI influenced their decision (**Smith**, 2007).

Many see the 'old' pre-1992 universities as more traditional and strict, catering to more middle-class white students and therefore less accessible to BME students from non-traditional educational backgrounds (Smith, 2007). BME students did not feel they would stand much of a chance of getting in, and made comments including 'it is way too out of my league!' Another factor determining whether they stay closer to home is economic. In the light of the tuition fees that students now have to pay, black and minority working-class students reduce their costs by not leaving home.

STUDENT MOTIVATION

Carrington and Tomlin (2000) found black and minority ethnic PGCE students' motivations for entering teaching are:

- disillusionment with other careers
- giving something back to the community
- desire to act as role models or advocates for black and Asian children.

Research by **Basit** *et al.* (2007) echoes this latter motivation, pointing to the value of schools having a diverse range of teachers from different ethnic backgrounds to reflect the pupil composition, provide positive role models for minority ethnic pupils to counter cultural stereotypes in the classroom, and also to bring the benefit of multi-lingual expertise. However many black and minority ethnic students and their parents are concerned about the reputation of teaching's low status. Racism was cited as a significant deterrent for electing not to go into teaching.

Many black teachers had gone to university and become teachers in part because of support from positive role models in their past, both black and white (**Pole**, 1999). Schools and career services can encourage students to consider teaching.

Many black and minority ethnic teachers come to teaching after pursuing careers elsewhere while also having established local ties and commitments (**Carrington** *et al.*, 2001). Support should be tailored to enable career transition and the financial hardships this may involve. Further research may be needed into how ethnic minority students cope with this transition.

RECRUITMENT STRATEGIES OF HEIs

In a study of minority ethnic students and HEIs, **Basit** *et al.* (2006) recommended that ITT institutions provide targeted support and think about the most appropriate routes into teaching, depending on a student's personal circumstances. For example, recruitment strategies should be matched with early intervention strategies at HEIs and schools, so those who enter teaching with lower grades can be given additional and targeted support. 'It is pointless to waste valuable resources on specialist advisers, coordinators and race officers, when the money can be more productively spent on training ITT tutors and school mentors to increase their knowledge and sensitivity to issues of race' (Basit *et al.*, 2006: 407).

Based on interviews with tutors in HEIs from institutions with relatively high levels of minority ethnic recruitment, **Carrington** *et al.* (2000) found the following strategies adopted by HEIs attracted more minority ethnic students on to PGCEs:

- targeted advertising in specialist minority press and media
- offering taster courses for under-represented groups, an approach more common among newer universities
- liaising with community organisations
- use of black music stations to promote courses
- promotion and marketing of HEIs to ensure they have a public image as a local provider that values equal opportunities, with a commitment to multiculturalism, regional identity and local community, as well as strategies directed towards specific ethnic and other groups.

PUBLICITY AND PROMOTION

Advertising and information to teachers and students should emphasise the role of black teachers in non-race specific ways (**Carrington** *et al.*, 2001). Although many do see themselves as role models who want to 'give back' to their communities, intrinsic satisfaction and non-race specific reasons are key determinants of black people becoming teachers.

Black teachers must come to be seen as the norm rather than special role models. For instance, black teachers have an important contribution to make in all-white schools. Advertising must also relate to current perceptions e.g. that issues of race awareness and incidents of racism will be dealt with appropriately.

LESSONS LEARNED

WHAT TO CONSIDER IN ORDER TO HAVE FAIR AND EQUAL ADMISSIONS AND RECRUITMENT

The case studies show us that the following are needed for a fair and equal admissions policy:

- An institutional culture in which admissions and recruitment are central to promoting race equality.
- Workshops to enable students to understand how to 'sell themselves', including preparation for the application and interview process.
- Trained tutors, sensitive to race equality issues, together with the student workshops, which will allow tutors to see where students are over-emphasising their weaknesses and under-emphasising their strengths.
- Utilising the experience of past students in the recruitment process. This has been done in many ways from mentorships and email exchanges to students speaking at open days and recruitment fairs.
- The external image of an institution is vital to its ability to attract a diverse range of students.
- Working alongside local schools and FE colleges will open universities up to a broader range of students. This can be done by holding more open access events such as open days or summer schools and publicising widening participation initiatives such as 'Aimhigher' or refugee access courses such as RiT (Refugees into Teaching).

ENDNOTES

1. ITE admissions are tied to Training and Development Agency requirements which stipulate a first degree. The reference to a minimum degree award refers to the classification awarded for the first degree (e.g. 2.2, 2.1, etc.).

CHAPTER 3
STAYING THE COURSE: RACISM, RETENTION AND PROGRESSION

DEALING WITH RACISM

How do you support students who experience racism during their course and teaching practice? Tutors saw this as a core concern that is central to the retention of black and minority ethnic students. The experience of racism, although not frequent, was not uncommon on courses. Teaching experience was often the place where tutors reported having to deal directly with incidents around faith-based and cultural differences that were perceived as racist by the students (see Good Practice Notes 3.1).

GOOD PRACTICE NOTES 3.1: DEALING WITH INCIDENTS

Tutors who exhibited good practice were consistent in how they approached issues of racism and cultural difference. Successful approaches included the following:

- Ensuring clear and open communication between tutors, the student and the school in order to manage any potential problems.
- Acting quickly when problems arise and discussing them immediately with line managers and other involved parties in authority.
- Support networks, usually involving students in the course tutor group were useful in stopping students from slipping through the cracks and in picking up problems before it was too late.
- A strategy that many identified as a necessary, but a last resort, was a willingness to deselect a mentor, a department or even a whole school if they were unresponsive to dealing with racist incidents. This effectively means discontinuing a school's, department's or mentor's partnership with the HEI until any issues identified are addressed.

Many tutors took a proactive approach to tackling racist incidents both on the course and in the classroom. These brief case studies give us an example of how tutors interpreted and negotiated individual situations.

CASE STUDY
CATE: A CASE OF ACTIVELY INTERRUPTING RACISM

Cate, a tutor on the PGCE primary course received an email from Kalila, a Muslim student in her tutor group who said she felt her mentor was treating her more harshly than the other beginning teachers (BTs) in the school. The mentor had made comments about Muslim girls being 'too passive and acquiescent to teach effectively'. Kalila was convinced that this was a case of racism. Cate asked Kalila to detail her experience in writing so that she could take it up with the school and offered to arrange for Kalila to finish her placement at another school. The tutor arranged to meet with the mentor to discuss the matter. He said that it had been his experience that Muslim women made poor teachers because they were too passive with the pupils and they let them walk all over them. He said that if he was harder on Kalila this was the reason. Cate explained that his views represented a racist stereotype and had no place in teacher training. He disagreed and insisted they were merely an accurate assessment of the Muslim women teachers he had encountered.

Cate called the school's head to inform her of the situation and to let her know that the student was moving to a new placement. The course leader wrote to the head saying that the situation violated the HEI's and the school's duty to promote racial equality, and that the decision had been made to de-select the school until the school could assure the HEI that not only was the mentor no longer involved in teacher training, but that the school had taken steps to prevent this situation arising in the future.

CASE STUDY
MARK: A CASE OF PROACTIVE COMMUNICATION

Mark, the course leader for the PGCE geography course, sent an email to all of students due to begin the course asking if they had any scheduling or location requirements that needed to be taken into consideration in assigning teaching placements. One of the students, Fatima, wrote back to him asking if she could be placed at a school where she would be allowed to observe her prayer times and where there would not be a problem with her wearing her hijab. Mark asked her if she could meet to discuss what type of accommodations she would like. When they met, Mark extended his hand to shake Fatima's hand and she politely refused, saying 'I'm sorry but in my culture it would be inappropriate for me to shake your hand'. Mark said that it was good that she had told him. He then asked her what kind of requirements she had in terms of a prayer space, how often and what length of time she would need for her prayers. Mark contacted the partner school liaison at the school he was hoping to send Fatima to and asked if the accommodations could be handled. The liaison said that they already had two prayer rooms set up for members of staff. Mark then asked about the hijab and told the liaison that Fatima could not shake hands with any male staff members. The liaison said that there would be no problem with the hijab and that he would explain to staff members not to expect Fatima to shake hands. Shortly after this Fatima began a very successful teaching practice at the school.

CASE STUDY
DIANA: A CASE OF CHALLENGING OVERT RACIST BELIEFS HEAD-ON

Diana, a white course tutor on the secondary PGCE, faced a challenging discussion about race and academic achievement with a group of ethnically mixed students. The students were reporting back on their school placements when Ned, an older white trainee, stated emphatically that in his school black boys were underachieving very badly because in his view, 'they are just not suited to academic work'. He explained he was only saying what he saw and had formed an opinion over a period of time based on observable evidence. He knew the theory of the self-fulfilling prophecy about teachers believing that black pupils won't achieve and therefore they don't. However, Ned felt this was a distraction because he was of the opinion that 'the same genes that affect your IQ affect your skin colour'. Another white female student agreed that there was a genetic explanation because 'why are 100-metres runners black and all the swimmers white?' Diana was not prepared for this discussion and felt intimidated by Ned's direct manner and confidence in his belief. On the one hand, she felt she did not have the detailed knowledge to challenge him and did not want conflict in her class. On the other hand, she had an ethnically diverse class and felt it was her duty to challenge him, which she began to do by unpicking his evidence. However the matter was soon taken out of her hands as Ned was robustly challenged by several of the students in the class. They openly stated that this was a racist view and everyone has the ability to learn. Ned got very upset and felt he was being picked on when he was just being honest.[1] Diana wrapped up the heated discussion with an offer of a reading list about racism and IQ. She also organised a special talk by an in-house expert on race and ethnicity which was well attended and addressed the issues on black underachievement raised by Ned.

CASE STUDY
MARY: A CASE OF BREAKING RACIAL BARRIERS THROUGH EMPATHY

Issues can be specific to the post-compulsory sector teaching not pupils but adult learners. An elderly learner may require different strategies and techniques to tackle hard and fast racist thinking. Mary, an 80-year-old white woman in an adult education centre was attending a reminiscence class with a racially diverse group of older retired women. Mary refused to sit next to people 'with a different skin colour', and asked the tutor if she could be seated away from the Asian and black members of the group. The trainee was in a dilemma. Does she treat an elderly person's racism differently to that of a young person? Should she try to 'understand' an older person's fears to difference and change? Should she avoid confrontation or address the issue head-on and risk upsetting the whole group dynamic? How should she employ her own ground rules of 'zero tolerance' towards racist sentiment without alienating fragile racial identities on all sides? The trainee had to think on her feet and quietly made the decision to allow Mary to sit as she pleased, away from the minority ethnic participants. The trainee was greatly troubled and took the issue back to her tutor. They decided on a long-term strategy. Their overall aim was to keep Mary in the class and open her to new experiences. The class entailed exchanging stories of the past, bringing food and sharing experiences. Uma, a 78-year-old woman, shared with the group her story of bereavement and family loss during the atrocities of Partition and the war between India and Pakistan. In the tea break Mary slipped in beside Uma and touched her arm, and said she too had lost family during World War II. They continued to chat and sat next to each other after the break. The trainee tutor structured in remembrances of migration and moving as a theme for the future so the issues of xenophobia and racism could be tackled more directly.

PROGRESSION, RETENTION AND CULTURAL DIFFERENCE

How do you tackle cultural, faith-based and familial tensions without being racist or patronising? Traditional restrictions and family responsibilities did impact on some students' achievement and ability to complete the course. Some tutors felt multiculturalism, which aims to be inclusive and accommodate different cultures and religions, can conflict with their aims of supporting students to achieve their potential. Others felt life episodes such as looking after sick parents and children can affect everyone in the same way, so providing flexibility to all students is important (see Good Practice Notes 3.2).

GOOD PRACTICE NOTES 3.2: GIVING SUPPORT

We found that successful intervention to support and retain black and minority ethnic students required the following:
- students needed to feel confident about telling tutors about their problems at home before tutors could offer constructive support
- black and minority ethnic students were more likely to approach tutors with problems if tutors were from a similar gender or minority group
- cultural, religious and familial traditions can affect students in different ways and may not always be constraining.

The following case studies show how tutors navigated these sensitive issues.

CASE STUDIES
YASMIN: A CASE OF RESOLVING CULTURAL TENSIONS

Yasmin, a Muslim student, was experiencing opposition from her family about doing the PGCE to become a secondary school teacher. Yasmin would mark her pupils' assignments at an underground station rather than go home. After consulting with Yasmin, her course tutor found her a room at the university halls of residence and arranged for her to see the counsellor at the university. She was put in touch with an Asian women's group who offered her culturally specific support. Her tutor also alerted the school to her situation. She felt strongly that the schools needed to know about aspects of students' lives such as tensions with religion and tradition or caring for parents or children that impacts on their achievements. Yasmin completed the course, increased her confidence and got a job.

BIRGUL: A CASE OF FLEXIBILITY AND FAMILY RESPONSIBILITIES

Birgul, a PGCE secondary student from Turkey, was living in London with her husband and two young children under the age of five. She mentioned to her tutor that her husband was quite traditional and childcare was a problem. She had no family networks here to support her during her school placement. The tutor was aware that many students with refugee, migrant or overseas backgrounds have potentially weaker support networks which can affect their participation level and therefore their likelihood to stay the course. However he wanted to accommodate and support Birgul, which meant she had to delay the school placement for several weeks. This raised many problems for the tutor and the school which they negotiated and overcame through dialogue and compromise. Birgul managed eventually to complete the course.

MEASURING IMPACT: RACISM, RETENTION AND ETHNIC MONITORING

While there are many concerns about ethnic monitoring being a 'tick box' exercise and a reinforcement of racial stereotypes through labelling (Bhavnani *et al.*, 2005), ethnic monitoring still remains a necessary tool to map patterns of black and minority ethnic recruitment, retention and progression (see Good Practice Notes 3.3).

GOOD PRACTICE NOTES 3.3: EFFECTIVE MONITORING

Ethnic monitoring provides an invaluable tool for HEIs to understand the effectiveness of their procedures. Effective ethnic monitoring includes:

- Explicit and clear reasons for undertaking the monitoring.
- The need for monitors and those being monitored to understand what the monitoring is aiming to achieve.
- The need for sensitivity to the ways in which racism and discrimination is not visible or apparent.
- The value of consistency in the categorisation used for the collection of national UK census data to enable more effective and powerful comparisons to be made.
- The importance of providing adequate training for the preparation, interpretation, analysis and communication of ethnic monitoring data.
- Avoidance of monitoring becoming a mechanistic activity by ensuring it is flexible, reflects and responds to particular local contexts (Menter *et al.*, 2003).

Tutors on the PGCE thought it was important to complement the qualitative data on staff and student experience with the statistical analyses derived from ethnic monitoring. They raised the following points:

- **Meeting targets**: Target setting is not in itself enough. If the prime focus of discussion about black and minority ethnic involvement in teaching revolves around meeting recruitment targets – without a similar discussion about retention and progression – the higher-than-average attrition rate that occurs among this group will remain invisible and unaddressed.

- **Good practice in ethnic monitoring**: Some PGCE courses developed a clear rationale for the way in which they would deal with issues of race, faith and culture. A designated member of academic staff was identified and acted as the conduit for the work. In one course the strategy involved students receiving a lecture on race in education prior to the completion of the ethnic monitoring forms. Students were better informed of the reasons why ethnic monitoring was important, and this resulted in an improved return rate. By frontloading the race equality course input they also found students were more confident and comfortable in raising race issues during the course.

- **Effective feedback from black and minority ethnic students**. Black and minority ethnic students rarely spoke candidly about their experiences on the course, and there are a number of reasons for this. However, it was possible for some tutors to gain effective feedback from black and minority ethnic students. For example, on one PGCE programme all black and minority ethnic students were offered an exit interview at the end of their course (i.e. after all assessment processes were complete). This interview facilitated discussion about student experience (both HEI and school-based), career plans and recommendations for the improvement of the course. PGCE tutors reported that these discussions were invaluable in accessing data that would otherwise remain hidden and led to improvements in understanding black and minority ethnic student experiences. These included:

    i) school issues (racism from pupils, parents and on occasion teachers)

    ii) institutional issues (inappropriate management of curriculum, i.e. depicting black and minority ethnic communities as victims, and tutors who were not confident in discussing issues of 'race')

    iii) the future destinations and aspirations of newly qualified teachers (NQTs) from black and minority ethnic communities.

WHAT THE RESEARCH SAYS

Basit *et al.* (2006; 2007) found that withdrawal rates by minority ethnic students on teacher training courses were higher than withdrawal rates among white majority ethnic trainees. Personal factors were ranked highest as reasons for withdrawal, followed by family, and then the ITE provider. They explored both tutors' and students' explanations for this. No tutor felt that ethnic minority trainees left for reasons specific to their race/ethnicity and none felt that there were significant gender variations in decisions to withdraw. However in contrast to their white peers, black and minority ethnic students first ranked family as the reason for withdrawal. More than a quarter of minority ethnic students cited that they needed more moral support, feedback, encouragement and academic support from their HEI and felt that their HEI could have been more understanding of workload, childcare commitments, and provide better communication and support.

Black and minority ethnic ITE students are often placed in the worst schools, get the most difficult placements and are therefore more likely to fail. Students highlight their school mentor and a lack of support as one of the main reasons of their withdrawal. They also point to pupils in school who have stereotyped them as teachers and report how they are often positioned as experts on racial matters or dealing with ethnic minority pupils, and regarded as cultural experts (**Jones et al.**, 1997; **Pole**, 1999; **WRECC**, 1999).

When **Carrington et al.** (2001) asked PGCE minority ethnic teachers to reflect on their experiences 41 per cent expressed anxiety about placements and 26 per cent reported incidents of racism in their placement schools. This racism came from pupils and teachers, in the classroom and in the staff room, including some parents commenting that they did not want their children to be taught by black teachers. The authors recommend that tutors assist black and minority ethnic students by showing sensitivity when arranging placements.

Ethnic minority trainees could be better prepared to deal with the range of situations that they may face in schools (Carrington et al., 2001). In particular foreign teachers are expected to adapt to great changes in pedagogy, discipline and culture with very little support (**Cole and Stuart**, 2005; **Singh**, 2002). Extended and intensive forms of mentoring may be particularly appropriate for these teachers who have to adapt to a new context.

In order to foster career development, placements should offer teachers a wide range of situations, including placing black teachers in schools in white areas (**Ross**, 2003). However, placements should be sensitive to needs and abilities, and trainees should be able to reflect on their own assumptions. For instance, fears of harassment in schools are often based on past experiences, and are not always borne out in placement schools. Such action must be complemented with appropriate monitoring and support of placement teachers so that problems can be dealt with quickly. Teaching institutions should formalise this process and develop joint procedures with schools (**Carrington et al.**, 2001; **Stuart et al.**, 2003; **Mead** 2006).

Ross (2003: 23) emphasised that black and minority ethnic teachers should not be assigned to 'curriculum ghettos, or expected to specialise in areas of "race"', because if 'they feel that their only opportunities for career development are in the areas of multicultural education or English as an additional language (EAL), then they will either become socially constructed into such roles, or they will leave the profession'. Teachernet, an internet resource for teachers, states that as a stand-alone subject, EAL can be perceived as having low status in terms of national training strategies. It is not a subject specialism in teacher training, and the amount of coverage in PGCE and other teacher training courses is variable.[2]

Specialisation in EAL ceased to be an option for trainee teachers in the 1990s, and while ITE providers are required to supply some form of 'on-campus' EAL education, the complexity and compactness of the 36-week ITE course, means that often EAL education is limited (Murakami, 2008). NALDIC (National Association for Language Development in the Curriculum) recognises that supporting pupils with EAL requires considerable specialist knowledge and skill. However, although the number of EAL learners in schools has risen by over 50 per cent since 1997, specialist teacher expertise in schools has become increasingly rare. Based on the TDA's 2009 survey of NQTs, only 30 per cent and 10 per cent of secondary and 29 per cent and 9 per cent of primary NQTs rated their training to work with learners with English as an additional language as good and very good respectively. Thus 60 per cent of both primary and secondary NQTs felt that their preparation to teach EAL students was less than good and accordingly could be classed as inadequate.[3]

LESSONS LEARNED

WHAT TO CONSIDER WHEN DEALING WITH RACISM, FAITH AND CULTURAL DIFFERENCE

The case studies show that the following ground rules are needed if we are to have an open and proactive approach to tackling racism and make reasonable and respectful accommodations in a multicultural setting.

- A racist incident is 'any incident which is perceived to be racist by the victim or any other person'. This definition of a racist incident is taken from *The Stephen Lawrence Inquiry* (Macpherson, 1999: recommendation 12). Thus if the person experiencing a situation perceives it to be racist it must be taken seriously and treated as such.

- When dealing with cultural difference, a guiding rule is to have practices, policies and provisions that do not disadvantage or treat any individual less favourably than others because of their (or your own) actual or perceived religion, belief or non-belief.

- A clearly outlined and practised complaints procedure means knowing exactly how complaints should be handled and ensuring that they are consistently addressed when they arise.

- Open lines of communication between the HE training institute, partner schools and beginning teachers or ITE students enable many issues to be proactively engaged with before they become problems.

- Deselection, while not ideal, can be a useful tool in getting schools, departments, and individual tutors to reflect on, assess and change their behaviours and actions. It is important to note that deselection of a partner institution need not be permanent, but a necessary step to protect students while changes are being made.

- Where possible and reasonable, appropriate services and accommodations should be provided to meet the cultural and religious needs of staff and students. This can include meeting food requirements where appropriate and practicable (e.g. halal, kosher, vegetarian), accommodating religious leave, and arranging for prayer space when necessary.

ENDNOTES

1. The expression of hurt and offence as a tactic of recentring 'whiteness' and white privilege in conversation is addressed in Chapter 5 (see also Aveling, 2006 and Applebaum, 2008).

2. See http://www.teachernet.gov.uk/teachingandlearning/library/EALteaching (accessed 11 November 2011).

3. See www.naldic.org.uk/ITTSEAL2/teaching/index.cfm (accessed 11 November 2011).

CHAPTER 4
PROMOTING DIALOGUE: DEVELOPING CURRICULUM AND RESOURCES

WALKING THE LINE: PROFESSIONAL CHALLENGES IN RACE, FAITH AND CULTURE

We are a community of practitioners that never share practice. We find it hard to get together. I would like to know how others do it and succeed!
(Secondary PGCE tutor)

Having 'space' to discuss and reflect on issues of race, faith and culture in a safe non-judgemental environment is crucial to embedding a true commitment to race equality among the course teams. However with heavy demands on tutors' time, finding such a space has difficult resource implications for HEIs. Some tutors talked of the importance of getting the right kind of space in order to deconstruct effectively their practice and pedagogy (see Good Practice Notes 4.1). As one post-compulsory tutor explained, it is not just what you discuss – it is how you discuss it. 'Talking about race and religion is hard. There is a danger of intellectualising issues to make them safe, which ends up closing down discussion so really important issues can end up on the shelf' (post-compulsory PGCE tutor).

GOOD PRACTICE NOTES 4.1: ADDRESSING DIVERSITY

Tutors' experiences and feelings about addressing diversity and difference highlights specific challenges such as:

- The need for institutional resources to provide adequate support to some black and minority ethnic students, without which there are restrictions in positively recruiting and retaining black and minority ethnic students.
- The different levels of diversity training for staff who have different levels of race and cultural awareness.
- The space for staff to voice their sentiments and explore some of the contradictions in dealing with diversity and difference.

An important challenge in addressing issues of race, faith and culture among teacher trainers on the PGCE is that it is ultimately about changing attitudes. Tutors often felt uncomfortable and unprepared to deal with the issues when they arise. When issues do arise, they are commonly dealt with in the space of informal individual conversations. Some tutors commented that they did not engage with the issues in open discussion because of their concern that it can be a contentious topic.

> When some of these issues come up, you are not ready for them and when they do come up you don't know how to handle them, and students don't want to raise them because they feel they will be written off as racist.
> (Post-compulsory tutor, discussion group)

> Tutors may be at different levels of confidence, understanding and engagement, so people will be feeling more insecure and others more secure.
> (Secondary tutor, interview)

RESOURCES FOR STAFF

The lack of resources to embed training for tutors to better equip them to deal with such discussions was a major problem, as the following points demonstrate:

- **Tutors spend unallocated and unaccounted-for time** dealing with issues of race, faith and culture. Many tutors are responding in their own time to resolve these issues. One primary tutor noted in a discussion group the problem with fitting all the training into nine months: 'Students need space to raise concerns and worries, reflect and grow, and issues [for black and minority ethnic students] very rarely arise until crisis point and that is when tutors frequently give their own time to try and resolve this.'

- **Having a space for discussion** would be a valuable time to reflect on practice as currently they are not given the opportunity to think 'critically about what diversity etc. means' (post-compulsory tutor, discussion group). While most tutors we spoke to said they would value having this space on a regular basis, it was also recognised that frequency, resources and time to have these spaces could prove to be the main hindrance.

- **Embedding the discussion groups institutionally** as part of team meetings would counteract the problem. Thus pitching the level of discussion is a key issue to consider and would require an experienced facilitator to carry forward the discussions. 'Training tends to be optional, and some tutors have been in this institution for a very long time…and wouldn't go to this low level training, they might feel insulted' (secondary tutor, interview).

CASE STUDIES
TAKING A RISK OR BEING OPEN?

Brian, a post-compulsory tutor, cited the example of a student initiating a debate about 'what is culture'. He had to deal with this spontaneously:

> I had an incidence that involved an in-depth discussion on what constitutes culture, because one of the students said: 'I feel sometimes that our culture is being eroded'. So we used that as a starting point to explore what we meant by culture. It was interesting that at the end there were white middle-class students who were feeling that their culture was being eroded and conceded in the end that their culture was being enriched and not eroded because we had an open discussion, where people from different ethnic groups and backgrounds were able to add to that...it is highly contentious...I would be careful about introducing that as a topic but at the same time know that we need to talk about it...Nobody told me how to deal with it but you come to know people and you just deal with it.

DIALOGUE, DIVERSITY AND DOUBLE STANDARDS

Julian, a secondary tutor, felt the need to have a space to voice his concerns about whether the HEI is a secular or multi-faith space and how 'faith' can be problematic and sometimes conflict with gender equality issues:

> I have problems with respecting faith-based knowledge – what is faith-based knowledge? Some of it for me is totally misogynistic, completely unpleasant, and I don't agree with or respect it – why should one respect faith-based knowledge per se? Religious holidays I don't have a problem with at all. What I am unsure about is whether this space is a secular space or not, and this has caused tensions that have been resolved but I am not really happy with the way they have been resolved. That needs greater discussion. I am not happy with the prayer room. If there is going to be a room, it should be one where people go to meditate and if people want to pray there that's fine. I did have a problem with the term 'prayer room' as it discriminates against people who have no faith and if this is a secular institution we should be tolerant and accepting of diversity but I think the prayer room does the opposite...the whole issue of faith is really problematic and I think having a mosque where to pray, a church, synagogue needs more discussion. There doesn't seem to be a problem with religion coming into secular spaces but when it is the other way round, then we are told we have to respect that space.

INTERSECTIONALITY[1] OF RACE, FAITH AND CULTURE

The contradictions that are regularly encountered when dealing with diversity and difference are in part due to how issues of race, faith and culture intersect with other issues. Tutors had to deal with complex issues related to gender, age, class and migrant status, alongside race, faith and culture:

> *There was one Muslim teacher who just wasn't prepared for teaching a group of large African Caribbean boys who can be quite aggressive and that wasn't part of her culture so for her that was a big step…to be able to develop her skills to deal with the guys that others may have had.*
>
> (Post-compulsory tutor, discussion group)

> *We had someone last year (Muslim female student), she…didn't want to be in an all-boys school or in a mixed school and we try to take this on board as with all other Equal Opportunities issues…The Muslim BT eventually said she would go to a mixed school but there was not much choice, as these were the arrangements here. In the end they offered her the job and she took it. She must have done some soul searching and gone for the better of the two evils between the mixed school and the boys school.*
>
> (Secondary tutor, interview)

> *There are eastern European students who have a different idea about what constitutes help and aren't prepared to accept support because that is seen as a failure…now we are looking at a multitude of different experiences and attitudes on our courses.*
>
> (Post-compulsory tutor, discussion group)

> *Black males are often isolated due to their very low numbers in ITE. My informal discussions with them indicate that they are often placed in the roles of 'the expert professional'…having insider knowledge to solve problems with black boys. At the same time they face a lot of hostility and can be excluded from staff room discussions. We cannot afford to lose them. Whilst we are developing robust systems which allow us to monitor student progress we have not yet got to a point where we track the academic progress of black and minority ethnic students on ITE courses. On the primary course we are able to do this to some degree, as part of our course monitoring, but I am not aware that this is widespread across secondary and post-compulsory PGCE.*
>
> (Primary tutor, interview)

CURRICULUM SOLUTIONS: WHAT THE TUTORS SAY

> *There is an issue about students being unfamiliar with the communities, faith, culture and differences in the schools they go into. I think we have to help them, and that can be a difficult journey for us all...We get the students to engage with the legal requirements, that is built into the course – for example the Race Equality duty, but that is policy. The next step is through practice.*
>
> (Secondary tutor, interview)

Issues of race, faith and culture are often addressed on a piecemeal basis on the PGCE. Tutors referred to the qualifying to teach standards (QTS)[2] with which they have to comply but which only loosely prepare all new teachers for teaching in a multicultural society. The standards are not prescriptive, leaving many trainee teachers without the practice and skills to deal with issues that arise with black and minority ethnic pupils in their classrooms. Often trainee teachers only have one or two hours on their teacher training courses on issues of diversity. It is only in particular subject areas or with particular tutors that students are encouraged to deconstruct and think about their experience or use a variety of resources that are meaningful to diverse learners. Tutors expressed a need for an embedded space to address issues of race, faith and culture in the curriculum. Raising these issues by running sessions early on in the course – that is, before students go into schools – is crucial. Tutors suggested this could take the form of:

- a yearly in-depth tutorial on multiculturalism
- setting coursework essays on multiculturalism and diversity
- continuous embedded discussion across subjects.

CASE STUDY
PROVIDING AN EMBEDDED DISCUSSION SPACE FOR STUDENTS

A diversity training session was held for secondary BTs from a variety of subject areas (Maths, English, Science and Languages). The session aimed to raise awareness on issues of race, faith and culture and support newly qualified teachers who have just completed their PGCE on issues of race, faith and culture. The three-hour session explored:

- The tensions and triumphs of working in multicultural learning and teaching environments.
- Sharing good practice between tutors and trainees to achieve a positive learning and teaching experience in diverse settings.
- How diverse students (BTs) can be best supported by tutors through their course and into schools.
- What tutors need to know about issues of race, faith and cultural difference.

BTs expressed apprehension about not feeling confident to start a debate with pupils, and that in a space such as the session it was valuable to hear other people's views and be able to discuss sensitive issues in a safe environment without being judged. All the students said that they would like to have a space to discuss race equality and diversity on a regular basis as they felt that BTs are often just left to find their way.

Sarah, a young white BT on placement in a mixed secondary comprehensive school in inner London, talked about the way she felt unprepared to deal with the day-to-day practicalities of teaching different religions. Sarah commented that she would have benefited from being briefed on the practices of different religions and cultures and on particular teaching areas to avoid. She related the following incident:

> I was doing a media lesson with Year 8 and the way women are represented in James Bond films so I looked at the character 'M', and I looked at a scene with Halle Berry, you know that scene when she comes out of the sea half-undressed and I had a Muslim girl in my class and she couldn't look at the screen. Now she was one of four Muslim girls in the class, and it became an issue and I became so annoyed that no one had told me, 'watch out for this', because I felt that I put her in a position. So I said look away and when it has passed I can give you a call to look back, and the white kids were saying that is stupid, why can't you look at it, and I was so annoyed…and I went to my manager and I said I am conscious that there are so many things that I am unaware of, of the day-to-day practicalities of the different religions and different cultures and races…I feel really inadequate, could you just tell me things to avoid now, the big minefields now…I felt completely out of my depth…I didn't know how to manage that.

CURRICULUM SOLUTIONS: WHAT THE STUDENTS SAY

When you teach in a London school you have 25 to 30 kids from different backgrounds in your class that each carry with them different assumptions, behaviours, expectations, customs, what have you, and that in itself, is going to affect the way you deal with those children regardless of your subject, because you are still dealing with human beings that you have to reach…race, culture, faith will have to be considered.

(Shannon, English BT)

Students said they would welcome the production of a good practice booklet to refer to when needed. This could cover how to approach issues that may arise with pupils and staff in schools; real case studies that tackle diversity; information dispelling myths about race and IQ; a list of key dates of religious festivals; teacher's language use, e.g. knowing what words to use. However students also recognised that simplistic inter-cultural 'top tips for teachers' is a limiting and problematic approach. Race, faith and culture are not just for and about black and minority ethnic people. Multiculturalism is a lived experience that is dynamic, interactional and constantly evolving for all concerned, whatever their race and ethnicity. There is no textbook with pat answers. It is important to have facilitated discussion groups that look at situations that are context-bound as one situation or school may be different from another (see Good Practice Notes 4.2).

GOOD PRACTICE NOTES 4.2: FACILITATING DISCUSSION

Student-centred facilitated sessions on race, faith and culture are about building confidence and providing an open forum for discussion of ideas and experiences. It could cover the following:

- 'what if' scenarios and real experiences, within and across subject areas
- ideas on how to respond to customs and restrictions that arise in the classroom including how to approach sensitive issues
- how to tackle teaching in a multicultural environment including what part children's culture and language plays in their learning
- what is diversity and how to implement it, including understanding how to tackle racism and racist bullying in schools (by teachers and pupils).

WHAT THE RESEARCH SAYS

Research by **Lander** (2011) on the racialised perceptions of white secondary school student teachers revealed their views about black and minority ethnic pupils were often cast in the language of 'otherness'. The inadequacy of student teachers' initial preparation to deal with the 'scary' situations associated with race issues in school had implications for curriculum and practice and in particular the institutional and school-based interface of ITE programmes. Lander suggests ITE needs to move beyond the skills-based standards and instead advocates an anti-racist CRT (critical race theory) framework that challenges students', tutors' and mentors' understanding about their own white ethnicity and how it is linked to 'everyday' racism and the perpetuation of white power structures. Wagner (2005) also advocates that student teachers need to be challenged within an anti-racist discourse. He suggests an accompanying meta-cognitive approach that provides a safety net for students to help them cope with the inevitable reactions of anger and denial they will experience.

Many teacher-training courses are wary of handling racism as an issue and race policies do not always filter through to organisational practices on the ground (**Robinson and Robinson**, 2001). For instance, students are not routinely trained in race awareness and incidents of racism are not always followed up. Only just over half of newly qualified teachers feel adequately prepared to teach pupils from diverse backgrounds (**TDA**, 2009). The TDA survey of newly qualified teachers (NQTs) shows that only 42 per cent of primary NQTs rated their preparation to work with learners from minority ethnic backgrounds as good or very good, and 38 per cent rated their preparation to work with learners with English as an additional language as very good or good. Forty-four per cent of secondary NQTs rated their preparation to work with learners from minority ethnic backgrounds as good or very good; and 40 per cent rated their preparation to work with learners with English as an additional language as very good or good (TDA, 2009).

Show Racism the Red Card (**SRtRC**, 2011a) conducted research to identify the barriers to tackling racism and promoting equality in schools. They found a significant lack of training for teachers, with 39 per cent of teachers never having received training in tackling racism or promoting equality. Of those who had, most felt the training was cursory and they felt ill-equipped to promote equality and tackle racism in the classroom. As a result of their lack of training many teachers appear to have adopted a 'colour-blind' position, where they try to ignore difference and are unsure about how to deal with racist incidents when they arise.

In a survey of ITE providers in England about the provision made to teach student teachers about diversity, **Davies and Crozier** (2006) found 97 per cent of providers had policies relating to equality. However these were not specific to student teacher preparation. The coverage of diversity issues was very variable, and providers interpreted the terms very narrowly. In most cases the term 'race' and ethnicity was seen to relate to the provision of pupils with English as an additional language and there was little coverage in terms of examining racisms and the impact of these on the lives of children. The education of refugees and asylum seekers, gypsy traveller pupils and the effects of social class or poverty were often omitted. The main constraints cited by providers in dealing with diversity were the lack of time, geographical location and the lack of commitment, knowledge and expertise within schools and among providers.

LESSONS LEARNED

Tutors and students had a wish list of good practice solutions for opening up institutional spaces for dialogue and curriculum development in race, faith and culture. It included the following:

- Difference and diversity should be embedded as a central aspect on the teaching programme rather than being an 'add-on'. Students on PGCE courses should be given a space to confidently explore race, faith and culture. This will enhance their learning experience and enable them to feel better equipped to deal with such issues when they arise on placement.

- Race equality issues should be integrated into team/course meetings where incidents could be regularly recorded and discussed. There could be cross-sector/phase meetings among tutors at the beginning of the year or once a term with a focus on race equality-themed issues for primary, secondary and post-compulsory. These sessions should stimulate discussion beyond simple compliance with the law, and help the teams clarify and explore their philosophy on difference and diversity.

- Special workshops for discussion and sharing good practice for tutors should be facilitated by someone experienced in race equality legislation, policy and practice. They should be a space where tutors can receive help to navigate the everyday minefield of multicultural classrooms and students. They should encourage tutors to think about difference more broadly, raising other issues such as class and gender. It could also be a space for discussions in the university as a whole, i.e. beyond PGCE.

- Universities or HEIs more broadly had much academic knowledge and expertise on equality and diversity that does not filter down to tutors and students on the PGCE. This could be done more effectively by breaking down silos of knowledge between academics who write about these issues and those who teach on ITE.

ENDNOTES

1. Intersectionality is a term coined in 1989 by the African American Critical Race theorist Kimberley Crenshaw (Phoenix and Pattynama, 2006). It rearticulates the scholarship of black feminists and represents a move away from the additive double or triple jeopardy models of race, class and gender in which one social position is ranked over another. Intersectionality provides a more complex understanding of the interlocking workings of race, class and gender and other social divisions such as sexuality, age, disability, ethnicity, culture, religion and belief. It refers to the systemic way in which social actors are simultaneously positioned in multiple structures of dominance and power as gendered, raced, classed, colonised, sexualised, disabled and aged 'others' (Mirza, 2009). It recognises that in reality we experience our gendered, racial and other identities in a continuous flow of one through the other. As Prins argues, 'gender is always lived in the modalities of ethnicity and class, and nationality in the modalities of gender and race, and class in the modalities of gender and nationality' (Prins, 2006: 278).

2. The new Teachers' Standards come into force on 1 September 2012 under the remit of the Teaching Agency. They replace the standards for Qualified Teacher Status (QTS) and the Core professional standards previously published by the TDA. There are no direct standards applying to the diversity of pupils except under Teachers Personal and Professional Conduct which state teachers must 'not undermine fundamental British values, including democracy, the rule of law, individual liberty and mutual respect, and tolerance of those with different faiths and beliefs' (DFE, 2011: 12). See: http://www.education.gov.uk/schools/teachingandlearning/reviewofstandards/a00192172/review-of-teachers-standards-first-report (accessed 11 November 2011).

CHAPTER 5

LOOKING IN THE MIRROR: USING THE LAW AND LEARNING ABOUT OURSELVES

DEVELOPING REFLEXIVE PRACTICE

Professional reflection is a major part of any attempt to improve retention and progression of black and minority ethnic students. Taking time to take stock of experiences, practices and biases among the course team is crucial to understanding what works best when dealing with students and partner schools. Reflection not only helps the retention of black and minority ethnic students, but it is vital to the success of the course as a whole in developing a new generation of diverse and well-rounded teachers. Using equality policy and legislative drivers to develop good practice had a positive and measured effect on retention and progression. Assessing good practice also provided tutors with a greater opportunity to deliver a more bespoke style of tutoring, and gave BTs and partner schools more tools for success.

The following examples demonstrate reflexive practice and professional development among the PGCE course teams.

WORKSHOPS FOR TUTORS

The PGCE primary course team organised a workshop for tutors in which they looked at past anonymised applications, as a means of reflecting on what they were valuing and what they were discounting during the application process. This was then used to evaluate how these processes shaped who was accepted onto the course and who was not in relation to ethnicity. Tutors felt that the workshop created a space in which it was safe to question their own practices, and this in turn led to the possibility for improvement. 'It helped us to re-evaluate our short-listing criteria, while at the same time helping many of my colleagues recognise that while many black and minority ethnic students don't come with the same footprint as some others, they do add a great deal of value to the course' (Karen, PGCE primary tutor).

BLACK AND MINORITY ETHNIC STUDENT GROUPS

The PGCE primary course team established a black and minority ethnic student group following the adoption of the Race Equality Policy. The group provided a space for black and minority ethnic students to reflect on their experiences of the course. This reflection served two purposes: it provided a support structure for the students involved, and served as guidance for the course tutors as they tried to reflect on their own practices.

Creating online communities for students also created opportunities for peer support, guidance and reflection. It provided a safe space for students to share their experiences and advise each other. This support is often vital to retention and progression. 'I find that the best support our students get is from each other' (Ian, tutor on the PGCE post-compulsory course).

MONITORING AND EVALUATION

In keeping with national requirements, PGCE courses keep a close track of statistics on the recruitment, retention and progression of black and minority ethnic students through their annual review process. Rather than monitoring being just a paper exercise, some course teams proactively used the statistics to strengthen recruitment, minimise drop-out and re-evaluate targets. This form of positive action allowed many of the PGCE courses to identify patterns and react quickly to shifts and new trends within crucial areas. 'We have all sorts of numbers on retention and when we have used them properly we have seen dramatic improvements' (Sarah, tutor on PGCE art and design).

CASE STUDY
VINCENT: A CASE OF POSITIVELY USING THE STUDENT EXPERIENCE

Vincent, a tutor on the PGCE modern foreign languages course, asked his students to write their own linguistic and educational biographies and to reflect on how these histories had shaped who they were and how they related to learning languages. It is a common practice on the PGCE to ask students to undertake this type of assignment. As the students began to think about their own histories they applied this knowledge to their pedagogy and to how they approached their teaching practice. Many of the students told Vincent it was as if a light went on for them. One student from a minority ethnic background, who had been struggling during his first classroom observation, was like a new person during his second observation. When Vincent asked him about the change, the student told him that the biography assignment had helped him make a connection between language learning and his own pedagogy that he had not made before. He also said that he had used the biography assignment with his own students to get them to think about how they approached his class as learners, and to get them to think about why learning another language might be useful and relevant to them.

Vincent added: 'In getting our students to reflect on their own histories and experiences, it becomes easier for them to see the importance of engaging with their own students' histories and experiences.'

HOW DO WE KNOW IF WE ARE GETTING IT RIGHT?

THE LAW

Equality legislation aims to tackle the roots of discrimination by laying down the principles and mechanisms that ensure everyone's right to be treated fairly and the opportunity to fulfil their potential. The Equality Act 2010 provides an overarching single legal framework that brings together 40 years of previous equality legislation.[1] This includes the watershed Race Relations Act (1976) and Race Relations (Amendment) Act (2000)[2] which are now 'harmonised' under the Equality Act (see Key Point Summary 5.1).

KEY POINT SUMMARY 5.1: THE EQUALITY ACT 2010

The Equality Act protects students from discrimination and harassment based on certain 'protected characteristics'. In further and higher education the **protected characteristics** are:[3]

- age
- disability
- gender reassignment
- pregnancy and maternity
- race
- religion or belief
- sex
- sexual orientation.

Being married or in a civil partnership is not a protected characteristic for the purposes of further and higher education.

A key measure in the Equality Act is the Public Sector Equality Duty.[4] The Public Sector Equality Duty (called the Equality Duty) replaces the previous the Race, Disability and Gender Duties. It ensures that public bodies, such as further and higher education institutions, consider the different needs of all individuals and their employees when shaping policy and delivering services. The Public Sector Equality Duty has three aims:

- to eliminate discrimination, harassment, victimisation and any other conduct that is prohibited by or under the Equality Act
- to advance equality of opportunity between persons who share a relevant protected characteristic and persons who do not share it
- to foster good relations between persons who share a relevant protected characteristic and persons who do not share it.

GOOD PRACTICE TOOLS FOR RACE EQUALITY

Good institutional practice for achieving race equality in HEI institutions includes adopting the following policy tools:

EQUALITY IMPACT ASSESSMENTS

An equality impact assessment is a way of systematically and thoroughly assessing, and consulting on, the effects that a proposed policy is likely to have on people, depending on their protected group. For example, the formal shift to an M-level PGCE[5] with the inclusion of Masters level elements on the course could be both positive (i.e. provide opportunities for Masters level learning and teaching) and negative for black and minority ethnic applicants (i.e. result in lower recruitment due to the upgrading of M-level admissions criteria). Formal equality impact assessments are no longer required by law[6] but are good practice and an important and powerful way to anticipate how changes in policy can impact on black and minority ethnic students (see Good Practice Notes 5.1). Equality impact assessments are a way of keeping a record of how decisions have been reached and is a way for public bodies to demonstrate that they meet the requirements of the Equality Duty.

GOOD PRACTICE NOTES 5.1: EQUALITY IMPACT ASSESSMENTS

An equality impact assessment in a HEI can ask:

- How will the changes affect admission requirements and will these changes strengthen or weaken the recruitment and retention of black and minority ethnic students?
- Will changes make the PGCE more or less accessible to students from non-traditional routes?
- How does this affect assessment? In relation to assessment does this process present an opportunity to broaden the criteria for success and give greater flexibility in recognising and valuing different skill sets?
- What other individuals and organisations are likely to have an interest in the proposed changes?
- Do these stakeholders include representatives from all the racial groups likely to be affected by the proposed policy?

COMMUNITY CONSULTATION AND PARTNERSHIP

Schools have an important role in promoting community cohesion and public organisations have a positive duty to promote good race relations by law.[7] This makes engagement with a wide range of educational and community stakeholders more than just good practice, but essential for providing an educational service that is 'fit for purpose' in a diverse, multicultural and multi-faith society. To establish positive and inclusive working relationships, as educational providers we need to ask:

- Do we consult local communities adequately about issues that concern them?
- Can we show that we have attended to their views and concerns?
- How do we work in active partnership with the communities we serve?

INSTITUTIONAL RACISM

Institutional racism refers to the process and effects of indirect organisational discrimination that disadvantages minority ethnic and protected groups in seemingly unconscious but insidious ways.[8] While good practice is crucial in framing the everyday tasks of tutors and the experiences of their students, tackling institutional racism goes beyond simply sharing good practice as a means of addressing racism. It has to involve a review of structures and practices that enable ingrained racist attitudes to persist in everyday practices. To address the insidious and 'unwitting' racism embedded in our organisational structures the governance of the institution needs to ask:

- Does our organisation work with an understanding that racism operates at a much more nuanced level than overt and identifiable bigotry?
- How is racism embedded in both the systems and policies of our institution?
- What are the discernable outcomes institutional racism produces?
- What is our institutional ethos and what are our leadership challenges in promoting good race relations?

POSITIVE ACTION

Positive action is action aimed at ensuring that people from previously excluded or disadvantaged minority ethnic or other protected groups can compete on equal terms with other applicants. It is intended to either prevent discrimination or make up for the accumulated effects of past discrimination. Positive action is not to be confused with positive discrimination or affirmative action, which is not legal. Good quantitative and qualitative evaluations of policies allows positive action to be taken to prevent discrimination and enable equality of opportunity for groups whose position can be affected by the cumulative effects of past discrimination. Targets and policies can be set if there is evidence of under-representation of minority ethnic groups within various levels of organisational practice, such as recruitment and retention or progression. Effective data collection can be developed by asking the following questions:

- How does our organisation monitor its own progress? Is it collecting appropriate and useful statistics?
- Is it keeping track of people's experiences, impressions and perceptions?
- Does the institution respond to the data appropriately?

CONTRACTUAL COMPLIANCE

It is common practice for further and higher education establishments to outsource many of its key activities and services. They are a vital part of the life of an HEI which can have contractual arrangements with a number of external partners such as catering, cleaning, reprographics, security services and partner schools. Under the Equality Duty it is essential that all contracts are examined for compliance. Public bodies are responsible for ensuring that any third parties who exercise functions on their behalf are capable of complying with the Equality Duty. Service providers and partners need to agree with the HEI's equality policy. In entering any external arrangement we need to ask:

- Does our organisation fulfil its duty to promote equality by requiring and enforcing the compliance of all of its contractual partners?
- How do we review and monitor if our external partners are complying with the equality duty, and what do we do if they are not?

WHAT THE RESEARCH SAYS

Different forms of racism require different forms of intervention. Racism can be characterised as biological, cultural, religious, institutional, situational (such as when resources like housing are scarce) or elite – that is, reproduced by those who are from the elite social classes, including politicians and the media (**Bhavnani** *et al.*, 2005). If the form of racism is not identified, cases may be inadequately and inappropriately responded to. Professional interventions based on race equality legislation are imbued with contradictions inherent in their development. For example, positive policies to reduce racism, notably anti-discrimination, have often developed in tandem with other politically motivated 'elite' racist policies, notably on immigration, asylum, nationality and criminal justice, where racism is deeply implicated and entrenched.

For Essed, racism is not only an ideology and a structure but also a process because 'structures and ideologies do not exist outside the everyday practices through which they are created and confirmed' (**Essed**, 1991: 44). Routine and repetitive practices help to maintain existing social structures and relations. These social practices and ideas are incorporated into the way people live their everyday lives. They are reflective of and reconstitute the deeper roots or causes of racism. These practices activate underlying power relations. It becomes the *norm* of the dominant group to see 'others' as different and inferior, particularly in relation to the colour of one's skin. These prejudices are frequently hidden and are not something *added* on to people's thinking and behaviour, but remain embedded in how we see the world.

Sara Ahmed (2007a; 2007b) argues that equality or diversity documents alone cannot remove racism from the institution. These documents constitute non-performative institutional speech acts. Thus a university making a public commitment *to diversity*, or an admission that they are non-racist and *for equality*, becomes a speech act that works precisely by *not* bringing about the effects it intends. She explains having a good race equality policy gets translated into *being good at race equality* – 'as if saying is doing' (Ahmed, 2007a: 595). For example, newer universities that are seen as 'diversity led' (as they have many students from ethnic minorities and lower socioeconomic backgrounds) present themselves as 'being diverse' without having to do anything. Simply 'being diverse' means new universities need not commit to 'doing diversity' (Ahmed, 2007b: 224). On the other hand the 'ideal' research-led 'sandstone' universities are elite precisely because they have an image that is not diversity-led. They use the language of globalisation and internationalism where diversity for them means appealing to a wide variety of diverse people across cultures. Ahmed explains, diversity here is not associated with challenging disadvantage, but becomes another way of 'doing advantage' (Ahmed, 2007b: 224). The significant disparity between universities' policy commitments and the experiences of black and minority ethnic staff suggests deep ongoing institutional barriers and discriminatory practices in the higher education sector (**Hey** *et al.*, 2011).

Critical race theory (CRT) argues that 'whiteness' is a position that involves the maintenance of white interests and white privilege. It does so by excluding non-whites and by denying that white people are racialised (**Gillborn**, 2008). By asserting that white ethnicity is only claimed by extremist groups, whiteness assumes the 'business-as-usual' silent domination that sustains the symbolic violence of everyday racism. This whiteness is evident in the 'soft' anti-racist/multicultural position taken up by white student teachers and tutors (**Lander**, 2011). For example, **Wilkins and Lall** (2010) found racist comments aimed at black and minority ethnic student teachers were perceived as 'unwitting prejudice' rather than racist. A comment such as 'did you have an arranged marriage' was normalised rather than been seen as racist because of the lack of intentionality in the comment. **Solomon** *et al.* (2005) found student teachers rejected notions of white privilege as did **Aveling's** (2006) study in which the examination of whiteness led to student hostility, defence and denial. **Gaine** (2001) asserts that if it did 'not hurt' then it did 'not work', alluding to the cognitive conflict associated with race awareness training and that without it there would be no shift in students' attitudes. **Applebaum** (2008) puts forward a model of social justice pedagogy which uses experience to critically challenge white students who claim they are oppressed by political correctness in the classroom.

LESSONS LEARNED

Sharing good practice within institutions should be sustained and incorporated into the PGCE course. Tutors suggested that this could be done by:

- Skilled facilitators collecting a range of scenarios and situations from tutors and students, and discussing with the group what would be an appropriate response.
- Drawing out both real and imagined ('what if') scenarios, where tutors could openly and safely address their fears.
- Adopting a 'process over tips' approach through a learning environment, where no set answers are given, to enable tutors to feel confident about handling situations.
- Accessing mainstream race equality training that goes beyond ITE, to understand the context of historical and global racism.

ENDNOTES

1. The Equality Act 2010 consolidates the numerous acts and regulations that formed the basis of anti-discrimination law in Great Britain. This includes nine major pieces of discrimination legislation, around 100 statutory instruments setting out rules and regulations and more than 2,500 pages of guidance and statutory codes of practice – such as the Equal Pay Act of 1970, the Sex Discrimination Act (1975), the Race Relations Act (1976), the Disability Discrimination Act (1995), the Employment Equality (Religion or Belief) Regulations (2003), the Employment Equality (Sexual Orientation) Regulations (2003), the Employment Equality (Age) Regulations (2006), the Equality Act (2006) and the Equality Act (Sexual Orientation) Regulations of 2007.

2. The racially motivated murder of the black teenager Stephen Lawrence in London in 1993 and the subsequent mishandling of the case by the police led to the Stephen Lawrence Inquiry in 1999. *The Macpherson Report* produced from this inquiry brought the concept of institutional racism into the public domain and led to the passing of the Race Relations (Amendment) Act 2000 (RRAA). The act placed a duty on all public bodies to proactively eliminate unlawful racial discrimination and promote race equality.

3. For specific guidance for higher education see ECU (Equality Challenge Unit). The public sector equality duty: *Specific duties for England Implications for higher education institutions* (ECU website: http://www.ecu.ac.uk/publications/files/psed-specific-duties-for-england-sept11.pdf/view). Also, see EHRC *What equality law means for you as an education provider: further and higher education* (2011) http://www.equalityhumanrights.com/advice-and-guidance/further-and-higher-education-providers-guidance/

4. The Equality Act 2010 introduced a public sector Equality Duty, which higher education institutions and the Higher Education Funding Council for England have to meet. The duty is underpinned by specific duties. In England these commenced on 10 September 2011 (ECU web http://www.ecu.ac.uk/publications/public-sector-equality-duty-specific-duties-for-england).

5. See http://escalate.ac.uk/3976 for pilot project evaluating M level PGCE (accessed 6 December 2011).

6. The Equality Duty does not impose a legal requirement to conduct an equality impact assessment. Compliance with the Equality Duty involves consciously thinking about the three aims of the Equality Duty as part of the process of decision-making (GEO, 2011: 4). See: http://www.homeoffice.gov.uk/publications/equalities/equality-act-publications/equality-act-guidance/equality-duty?view=Binary

7. The Education and Inspections Act 2006 placed a duty on schools to promote community cohesion. This is now under consideration. See http://www.guardian.co.uk/education/2010/oct/20/community-cohesion-off-ofsteds-agenda; www.teachernet.gov.uk/wholeschool/community cohesion/ For a guide to good partnerships, see Runnymede Trust (2002).

8. Institutional racism is defined as: 'the collective failure of an organisation to provide an appropriate and professional service to people because of their colour, culture, or ethnic origin. It can be seen or detected in processes, attitudes and behaviour which amount to discrimination through unwitting prejudice, ignorance, thoughtlessness and racist stereotyping which disadvantage minority ethnic people. It persists because of the failure of the organisation openly and adequately to recognise and address its existence and causes by policy, example and leadership. Without recognition and action to eliminate such racism it can prevail as part of the ethos or culture of the organisation. It is a corrosive disease' (Macpherson, 1999: 28).

CHAPTER 6
CONCLUSION: CHALLENGING PERCEPTIONS AND CHANGING CULTURE

FACILITATING AN OPEN DISCUSSION ON RACE, FAITH AND CULTURE

> *This project is a step in the right direction. It has moved us to deal with something in a more coherent and structured way than we have been doing in the past. It is a good starting point but it is something that we need to reflect on constantly and do more, and now you start to realise that there are other things that you have to do.*
>
> (Secondary PGCE tutor)

The 'Respecting Difference' project is not only about sharing what is good practice, it is also about facilitating an open discussion among colleagues that can lead to the identification of hidden race equality issues in an organisation. It is important to understand that tackling institutional racism goes beyond an understanding of day-to-day good practice. While tutors may share good practice among themselves, they also work within organisational structures and policy regimes that have implicit and covert racist outcomes and effects beyond their immediate reach. The complex interplay of different social locations where minority ethnic students face racism means that sometimes the problems with recruitment and retention cannot be addressed solely through improved tutor practice and understanding. For example, students may also have lack of support from school mentors, stereotyping and racial abuse from pupils when on placements, as well as difficult conditions at home which can make recruitment and retention of black and minority ethnic students a complicated process.

Teacher educators in this book raised issues of key concern such as **'How do you tackle cultural, faith-based and familial tensions without being racist or patronising?'**

- Some tutors felt multiculturalism, which aims to be inclusive and accommodate different cultures and religions, can conflict with their aims of supporting students to achieve their potential.
- Others felt life episodes such as looking after sick parents and children can affect everyone in the same way, so providing flexibility to all students is important regardless of ethnicity.
- Tutors wanted more open dialogue in their institutions about tackling issues of racism at a personal and professional level if they were to be effective in supporting their black and minority ethnic students through their programmes of learning.

- Several tutors commented on their reluctance to take explicitly 'affirmative action' that might lead to the 'dilution of quality'.

Students in this study stated successful multicultural intervention required the following:

- Students need to feel confident about telling tutors about their problems at home before tutors can offer constructive support.
- Black and minority ethnic students were more likely to approach tutors with problems if tutors were of a similar gender or minority group.
- Cultural, religious and familial traditions can affect students in different ways and may not always be constraining.

Research identifies several key areas that are essential to successfully achieve race equality and educational inclusion. These are:

- Embedding multicultural and anti-racist teacher training.
- Developing inclusive classroom pedagogy with culturally relevant curricula.
- Enhancing race equality and diversity through challenging professional practice and leadership.

RECOGNISING RACISM: FLASHPOINTS IN INSTITUTIONAL PRACTICE

An important aim of this guide to good practice has been to address the hidden and less acknowledged ways in which racism operates by identifying and locating the institutional 'flashpoints' where black and minority ethnic trainees in an HEI may face discrimination and be disadvantaged because of their race, faith or culture. Searching and challenging questions need to be asked by the course teams to locate possible barriers to recruitment, retention and progression of black and minority ethnic students. Flashpoints identified in this study included:

- **The image and reputation of the ITE provider**: Is the HEI perceived as a white space or a privileged place by BME students? Is there fair and equal access for BME students?
- **Admission processes**: Who are the gate-keepers? What are their assumptions about the quality, ability and potential hurdles of BME students? How does this impact on their chances of recruitment?

- **Race equality awareness and anti-racist training**: How confident and skilled are tutors in dealing with race equality issues? What are the institutional resources for race equality training and the spaces for informal course reflection?
- **Course monitoring**: Is the recruitment and progression of BME students regularly tracked on courses? How is the data used, reviewed and fed back? Are there exit interviews for BME students?
- **Curriculum and pedagogy**: How are diversity, multiculturalism, bilingualism and multi-lingualism, and inclusive education approached in the ITE curriculum? Is it embedded or an add-on? Are all students confident in issues of race, faith and culture when they go out on a placement or when they graduate?
- **Placements in schools**: Do tutors liaise effectively with partner schools on BME progress? Are schools aware of the HEI's race equality policy and practice? What policies and practices are in place to support students of different race, faith and culture?

RECOGNISING RACISM: DEVELOPING GOOD PRACTICE

Developing an anti-racist perspective means addressing the hidden and less acknowledged ways in which racism operates. Tutors found the institutional culture around addressing issues of race, faith and diversity oppressive for good practice. The solutions they suggested included:

- Race equality issues to be integrated into team/course meetings where incidents could be regularly recorded and discussed. These sessions should stimulate discussion beyond simple compliance with the law, and help the teams clarify and explore their philosophy on difference and diversity. These discussion sessions could be used as a platform for how to take things forward at an institutional level.
- Institutions need to equip their PGCE teaching staff with clear policies and procedures including a clearly outlined and practised complaints procedure and clarification of who is responsible for what within their organisation, e.g. equal opportunities officers, race equality facilitators etc.
- Recruitment of students from diverse and non-traditional backgrounds could be increased by institutional recognition of the time staff need to provide targeted support and mentoring.

- Training to give students on PGCE courses a space to confidently explore race, faith, and culture, which enables them to feel better equipped to deal with such issues when they arise on placements.

RACE EQUALITY GOOD PRACTICE IN ITE: THE BIGGER PICTURE

- **'Teachers for the 21st century'** is a project that brings together ITT providers from the Yorkshire and Humberside region into a consortium, allowing them to pool their resources to address a shared philosophy to develop trainees as reflective practitioners. The model for partnership working that they have developed could be used to share good practice for supporting BME students across institutions (Leeds University, 2003).

- **Merseyside Black and Minority Ethnic Steering Group** is a consortium of Merseyside universities that jointly held a conference at Liverpool Hope University to address the recruitment and retention of black and minority ethnic trainee teachers in the North West region. The conference looked at barriers, perceptions and sharing good practice such as working with schools to encourage more pupils to embark on a career in teaching, such as the Somali/BME TASTE programme.[1]

- **Black Teachers in London** (2006), a report commissioned for the GLA (Greater London Authority) by the Mayor of London, recommends developing London-wide guidance on the recruitment, development and progression of black teachers with targets and monitoring in each LEA. It also favours race awareness training for all teachers and governors as well as fostering diversity on governing bodies. It suggests Ofsted should incorporate race equality into its criteria more explicitly. Another option is customised leadership development, which might help to raise cultural issues, address barriers and give extra support.

- **Show Racism the Red Card**, a campaign that uses top footballers to educate against racism, has produced a booklet, *Guidance for initial teacher trainers in preparing student teachers to tackle racism and promote equality in the classroom* (SRtRC, 2011b). It is aimed at ITT providers to comply with equality legislation and give them confidence to promote anti-racist professional practice among their students. The resource pack has practical activities and case studies for teacher trainers to use to prepare student teachers to tackle racism in the classroom. The project has been supported by NUT and NASUWT and funded by the Department of Communities and Local Government.

- **Multiverse** was an initial teacher-training professional resource network funded by the TDA. The website provided access to the latest research, news and best practice for teacher educators and student teachers to help them address the educational achievement of pupils from diverse backgrounds, including issues of social class, race and ethnicity. All materials, including commissioned research, was quality assured through a rigorous process of academic scrutiny by a team of expert teacher educators. The website, which had 900 entries and over 12,000 hits a month, closed in March 2011 but was an indispensible source of information among ITE providers and their students and still represents a model of excellent practice.[2]

- The **National Children's Bureau** publication *Young Children and Racial Justice* (Lane, 2008) is a resource aimed at in-house training and the day-to-day situations that may arise within all types of early years provision for practitioners and ITE trainers. It is a 'How to' book and gives sound, easy-to-follow advice for tackling the different aspects of racism and prejudice. There is a section relating to Travellers, Roma, Gypsies and mobile communities and how these, along with asylum-seekers and refugees, are often overlooked. The chapters cover a number of essential areas that not only enable practitioners to enhance their care and education of the children but also relationships with parents and other carers, outside agencies, team working and how all these areas can be approached from the aspect of racial equality.

- **Refugees into Teaching (RiT)** is a national TDA-funded project at the Refugee Council that supports getting overseas-trained refugee teachers into jobs in education in the UK. There are over 700 'refugee teachers' currently registered with the project nationally. The project works with partner organisations to build capacity and confidence in the English education system by providing access into training, work placements, and employment for refugee teachers.[3]

INTERSECTIONALITY OF RACE, FAITH AND CULTURE WITH GENDER, CLASS, SEXUALITY, DISABILITY AND AGE

We hope that the various cases presented will also assist readers in reflecting upon the issues affecting minority ethnic students that extend beyond race, ethnicity, faith and culture, to appreciate the complexity of experiences. For example, gender, class, sexuality, disability and age are important dimensions when looking at ways to improve the recruitment and retention of black and minority ethnic students. As we have seen, race, faith and culture manifest themselves in different ways depending on the students' gender, class, age, sexuality and disability. Thus the needs and support for Fatima, a young Muslim woman with religious restrictions is very different than for Majid, an older Muslim man with disabilities. The overarching category 'black and minority ethnic' – a post-colonial classification used to identify people of colour – subsumes complex differences among ethnic groups and as such can be too simplistic. For example, many trainees collectively categorised as black and minority ethnic state they are 'mixed race' and that the complexity of their identities is often overlooked.

To advance an intersectional approach we also need more data on the cross-cutting experiences of black and minority ethnic students according to the type of institution, e.g. older or newer university and location and region. We need to know where black and ethnic minority students are located in terms of subject specialism, type of educational institution and type of course – i.e. primary, secondary, post-compulsory. It is important to ask what is the drop-out rate of black and minority ethnic trainees in relation to these factors.

TOWARDS ANTI-RACIST DIALOGUE IN ITE

It is hoped the good practice recorded in this book will encourage anti-racist dialogue in ITE to enable us to better support our black and minority ethnic students through their programmes of learning and teaching. The tutors' reflections and insights openly shared with us in making this book show how tackling issues of race, faith and culture at a personal and professional level is an important aspect of changing racialised micro-institutional practices that can affect the recruitment, retention and progression of black and minority ethnic trainee teachers. The tutors' narratives in the case studies demonstrate the multiple and often contradictory challenges they face when supporting students from a range of ethnic, religious and cultural backgrounds. Anti-racist good practice in ITE is essential if a new generation of well-rounded black and minority ethnic teachers from diverse backgrounds are to justly fulfil their potential as teachers and educational leaders of what is now a diverse and multicultural British society.

ENDNOTES

1. See: Black and Minority Ethnic Teacher Recruitment and Retention Conference, 10 February 2010 http://www.hope.ac.uk/education-news/bme-conference.html (accessed 11 November 2011).

2. An archived snapshot of the site is available at: http://webarchive.nationalarchives.gov.uk/20101021152907/http://www.Multiverse.ac.uk/ (accessed 11 November 2011).

3. See: RiT, 2011 http://refugeesintoteaching.org.uk/impactreport (accessed 11 November 2011).

RESOURCES

In putting the book together, institutional policies such as Equal Opportunities and Race Equality Policies were extensively drawn upon, as was external guidance from groups including the Government Equalities Office (GEO), Equalities and Human Rights Commission (EHRC), the Runnymede Trust, the National Union of Teachers (NUT) and the Equality Challenge Unit (ECU).

MORE GUIDANCE CAN BE FOUND AT THE FOLLOWING LOCATIONS:

RESOURCES FOR GOOD PRACTICE

The Centre for Ethnicity and Racism Studies, Leeds – Institutional Racism in Higher Education Toolkit
www.leeds.ac.uk/cers

The Forum Against Islamophobia and Racism – Resources
www.fairuk.org/useful.htm

The General Teaching Council for England
www.gtce.org.uk/networks

Multiverse *Guidance on Equality Strategies, Promoting Race Equality and Cultural Diversity*, archived site still accessible at:
http://webarchive.nationalarchives.gov.uk/20101021152907/http://www.Multiverse.ac.uk/

The National Union of Teachers: Equal Opportunities Resources
www.teachers.org.uk

Show Racism the Red Card (2011). *Guidance for Initial teacher trainers: preparing student teachers to tackle racism and promote equality in the classroom*
www.theredcard.org

OFFICIAL GUIDANCE ON RACE EQUALITY, RELIGION AND BELIEF

The Equality and Human Rights Commission's Guidance for Education and Training Providers on Rights, Equality, Discrimination and the Race Equality Duty
www.equalityhumanrights.com

The European Commission Against Racism and Intolerance Policy Recommendations
http://www.coe.int/t/dghl/default_en.asp

The Runnymede Trust's Guidance on Racist Violence
www.runnymedetrust.org/uploads/publications/pdfs/PreventingWP.pdf

The Runnymede Trust's Guidance on Widening the Talent Pool
www.runnymedetrust.org/uploads/publications/pdfs/
wideningTheTalentPool.pdf

The Runnymede Trust's guide to promoting race equality in schools, *Complementing Teachers*
http://www.runnymedetrust.org/projects/education/resources-for-schools/
complementing-teachers.html

Equality Challenge Unit Guidance on Promoting Good Campus Relations, Dealing with Hate Crimes and Intolerance
http://www.universitiesuk.ac.uk/Publications/Documents/
promotinggoodrelations.pdf

Higher Education Equal Opportunities Network (HEEON)
http://www.heeon.ac.uk/

REFERENCES

Adonis, A. (2008) Parliamentary Under-Secretary of State for Schools and Learners Department for Children, Schools and Families. Speech delivered at the Initial Teacher Training Provider Conference on Diversity and Personalisation, 7 May 2008.

Ahmed, S. (2007a) 'You end up doing the document rather than doing the doing: Diversity, race equality and the politics of documentation'. *Ethnic and Racial Studies*, 30(4), 590–609.

Ahmed, S. (2007b) 'The language of diversity'. *Ethnic and Racial Studies*, (30)2, 235–56.

Applebaum, B. (2008) '"Doesn't my experience count?" White students, the authority of experience and social justice pedagogy'. *Race, Ethnicity and Education*, 11(4), 405–14.

Aveling, N. (2006) 'Hacking at our very roots: Rearticulating white racial identity within the context of teacher education'. *Race, Ethnicity and Education*, 9(3), 261–74.

Bariso, E.U. (2001) 'Code of professional practice at stake? Race, representation and professionalism in British education'. *Race, Ethnicity and Education*, 4(2), 167–84.

Basit, T.N., Roberts, L., McNamara, O., Carrington, B., Maguire, M. and Woodrow, D. (2006) 'Did they jump or were they pushed: Reasons why minority ethnic trainees withdraw from initial teacher training courses'. *British Educational Research Journal*, 32(3), 387–410.

Basit, T.N., McNamara, O., Roberts, L., Carrington, B., Maguire, M. and Woodrow, D. (2007) 'The bar is slightly higher: The perception of racism in teacher education'. *Cambridge Journal of Education*, 37(2), 279–98.

Bhavnani, R., Mirza, H.S. and Meetoo, V. (2005) *Tackling the Roots of Racism: Lessons for Success*. Bristol: Policy Press.

Bielby, G., Sharp, C., Shuayb, M., Teeman, D., Keys, W., and Benefield, P. (2007) *Recruitment and retention on Initial Teacher Training: A systematic review, final report*, November, National Foundation for Educational Research.

Black Teachers in London (2006) *A report for the Mayor of London* by Maylor, U., Ross, A., Rollock, N., and Williams, K. London: Greater London Authority.

Bush, T., Glover, D. and Sood, K. (2006) 'Black and minority ethnic leaders in England: A portrait'. *School Leadership and Management*, 26(3), 289–305.

Carrington, B., Bonnett, A., Nayak, A., Skelton, C., Smith, F., Tomlin, R., Short, G., and Demaine, J. (2000) 'The recruitment of new teachers from minority ethnic groups'. *International Studies in the Sociology of Education*, 10(1), 3–22.

Carrington, B. and Tomlin, R. (2000) 'Towards a more inclusive profession: teacher recruitment and ethnicity'. *European Journal of Teacher Education*, 23(2), 139–57.

Carrington, B., Bonnett, A., Demaine, J., Hall, I., Nayak, A., Short, G., Skelton, C., Smith, F., and Tomlin, R. (2001) *Ethnicity and the Professional Socialisation of Teachers*. Report to the Teacher Training Agency.

Carrington, B. and Skelton, C. (2003) 'Re-thinking "role models": Equal opportunities in teacher recruitment in England and Wales'. *Journal of Education Policy*, May–June, 18(3), 253–65.

Cole, M. and Stuart, J. (2005) '"Do you ride on elephants" and "Never tell them you're German": The experiences of British Asian and black, and overseas student teachers in South East England'. *British Educational Research Journal*, 31(3), 349–66.

Davies, J. and Crozier, G. (2006) 'Tackling diversity in ITE: Unpacking the issues'. *Race Equality Teaching*, 24(3), 18–21.

DFE (2010) Department for Education (2010) Statistical First Release: Schools, pupils and their characteristics, January. Online. http://www.education.gov.uk/rsgateway/DB/SFR/s000925/sfr09-2010.pdf (accessed 31 October 2011).

DFE (2011a) Department for Education Statistical First Release: Schools, pupils and their characteristics, January. Online. http://www.education.gov.uk/rsgateway/DB/SFR/s001012/sfr12-2011.pdf (accessed 31 October 2011).

DFE (2011b) Department for Education First Statistical Release, School workforce in England, November (provisional). Online. http://www.education.gov.uk/rsgateway/DB/SFR/s000997/sfr06-2011v4.pdf (accessed 31 October 2011).

Dingus, J.E. (2008) '"I'm Learning the Trade": Mentoring networks of black women teachers'. *Urban Education*, 43(3), 361–77.

Essed, P. (1991) *Understanding Everyday Racism: An Interdisciplinary Theory*. London: Sage Publications.

Fredman, S. (2001) *Discrimination and Human Rights: The Case of Racism*. Oxford: Oxford University Press.

Gaine, C. (2001) '"If it's not hurting it's not working": Teaching teachers about "race"'. *Research Papers in Education*, 16(1), 93–113.

Ghuman, S. (1995) *Asian Teachers in British Schools: A Study of Two Generations*. Clevdon: Multi-Lingual Matters.

GEO (2009) *A Fairer Future: The Equality Bill and other action to make equality a reality*. Crown copyright 2009. Online. http://www.homeoffice.gov.uk/publications/ (accessed 11 November 2011).

Gillborn, D. (2008) *Racism and Education: Coincidence or Conspiracy?* London: Routledge.

Harris, A., Muijs, D. and Crawford, M. (2003) *Deputy and Assistant Heads: Building Leadership Potential*. Nottingham: NCLS.

Hey, V., Dunne, M., Aynsley, S., Kimura, M., Bennion, A., Brennan, J., and Patel, J. (2011) *The experience of black and minority ethnic staff in higher education in England*, Equality Challenge Unit. Online. http://www.admin.cam.ac.uk/offices/hr/equality/documents/bme_experience.pdf (accessed 11 November 2011).

House of Commons (2010) Children Schools and Families Committee Report. *Training of Teachers*. Fourth Report of Session 2009–10, Volume 1 Report, together with formal minutes. London: The Stationery Office (HC 275-I).

Housee, S. (2004) 'Unveiling South Asian female identities' in I. Law, D. Phillips and L. Turney (eds), *Institutional Racism in Higher Education*. Stoke on Trent: Trentham Books, 59–70.

Jones, C., Maguire, M. and Watson, B. (1997) 'The school experience of some minority ethnic students in London schools during Initial Teacher Training'. *Journal of Education for Teaching*, 23(2), 131–44.

Lander, V. (2011) '"Race, culture and all that": An exploration of the perspectives of white secondary student teachers about race equality issues in their Initial Teacher Education', *Race, Ethnicity and Education* 3(14), 351–64.

Lane, J. (2008) *Young children and racial justice: Taking action for racial equality – Understanding the past, thinking about the present, planning for the future*. London: National Children's Bureau.

Leeds University, (2003) *ITT for the 21st Century: Project 10. FINAL REPORT* Teacher Training Agency Yorkshire and the Humber Region Partnership Promotion Project, S. Whitelaw, A. Hobson, N. Mitchell.

Macpherson, W. (1999) *The Stephen Lawrence Inquiry*. Cm 4262-I. (London, The Stationery Office). Online. http://www.archive.official-documents. co.uk/document/cm42/4262/sli-47.htm (accessed 6 December 2011).

Maylor, U., Dalgety, J. and Ross, A. (2003) *Minority Ethnic Teachers in England*. London: GTCE.

McNamara, O., Howson, J., Gunter, H. and Fryers, A. (2010) *The leadership aspirations and careers of black and minority ethnic teachers*, NASUWT and National College for Leadership of Schools and Children's Services. Online. http://www.nasuwt.org.uk/consum/groups/public/@equalityandtraining/ documents/nas_download/nasuwt_005377.pdf (accessed 11 November 2011).

Mead, N. (2006) 'The experience of black African religious education trainee teachers training in England'. *British Journal of Religious Education*, 28(2), 173–84.

Menter, I., Hextall, I. and Mahoney, P. (2003) 'Rhetoric or reality? Ethnic monitoring in threshold assessment of teachers in England and Wales'. *Race, Ethnicity and Education*, 6(4), 307–29.

Mirza, H.S. (1997) *Black British Feminism: A Reader*. London: Routledge

Mirza, H.S. (2009) *Race, Gender and Educational Desire: Why Black Women Succeed and Fail*. London: Routledge.

Murakami, C. (2008) '"Everybody is just fumbling along": An investigation of views regarding EAL training and support provisions in a rural area'. *Language and Education*, 22(4), 265–82.

Osler, A. (1997) *The Education and Careers of Black Teachers: Changing Identities, Changing Lives*. Buckingham: Open University Press.

Phoenix, A. and Pattynama, P. (2006) 'Editorial: special issue on intersectionality'. *European Journal of Women's Studies*, 13(3), 188–92.

Platt, L. (2011) *Understanding Inequalities: Social Stratification and Difference*. Cambridge: Polity.

Pole, C. (1999) 'Black teachers giving voice: Choosing and experiencing teaching'. *Teacher Development*, 3(3), 313–28.

Pole, C. (2001) 'Black teachers: Curriculum and career'. *The Curriculum Journal*, 12(3), 347–64.

Portelli, J. and Campbell-Stephens, R. (2009) *Leading for Equity: Investing in Diversity Approach*. Toronto: Edphil Books.

Powney, J., Wilson, V., Hall, S., Davidson, J., Kirk, S., Edward, S., SCRE Centre and Mirza, H.S. (2003) *Teachers' careers: the impact of age, disability, ethnicity, gender and sexual orientation*, Research Report 488. London: DfES.

Prins, B. (2006) 'Narrative accounts of origins: A blind spot in the intersectional approach.' *European Journal of Women's Studies*, 13(3), 277–90.

Reay, D., David, M. and Ball, S. (2005) *Degrees of Choice: Social Class, Race and Gender in Higher Education*. Stoke on Trent: Trentham Books.

Robinson, I. and Robinson, J. (2001) 'Sometimes it's hard to get a taxi when you are black: The implications of the Macpherson Report for teacher education'. *Journal of In-Service Education*, 27(2), 303–21.

Ross, A. (2003) *Ethnic minority teachers in the teaching workforce*, Institute of Policy Studies, Occasional Paper. London: London Metropolitan University.

Runnymede Trust (2002) *The Guardians of Race Equality: Perspectives on inspection and regulation*. Online. http://www.runnymedetrust.org/publications/15/32.html (accessed 6 December 2011).

Singh, V. (2002) *Managing diversity for strategic advantage*. Report to the Council for Excellence in Management and Leadership.

Siraj-Blatchford, I. (1991) 'A study of black students' perceptions of racism in Initial Teacher Education'. *British Educational Research Journal*, 17, 35–50.

Smith, H. (2007) 'Playing a different game: the contextualised decision-making processes of minority ethnic students in choosing a higher education institution'. *Race, Ethnicity and Education*, 10(4), December, 415–37.

Solomon, R.P., Portelli, J.P., Daniel, B.J. and Campbell, A. (2005) 'The discourse of denial: how white teacher candidates construct race, racism and "white privilege"'. *Race, Ethnicity and Education*, 8(2), July 2005, 147–69.

Solórzano, D.G. and Yosso, T.J. (2002) 'Critical race methodology: Counter-storytelling as an analytical framework of education research'. *Qualitative Inquiry*, 8(1), 23–44.

SRtRC (2011a) (Show Racism the Red Card) *Guidance for Initial Teacher Trainers: Preparing student teachers to tackle racism and promote equality in the classroom*. Online. http://www.srtrc.org/uploaded/ITT%20ED%20PACK.pdf (accessed 11 November 2011).

SRtRC (2011b) (Show Racism the Red Card) *The barriers to challenging racism and promoting race equality in England*. Online. http://www.srtrc.org/uploaded/SRTRC%20BARRIERS.pdf (accessed 11 November 2011).

Stuart, J., Cole, M. with Birrell, G., Snow, D. and Wilson, V. (2003) *Minority ethnic and overseas student teachers in South East England: An exploratory study.* Report to the Teacher Training Agency.

Swann Report. DES (1985) *Education for All. Final Report of the Committee of Inquiry into the Education of Children from Ethnic Minority Groups.* London: HMSO.

TDA (2009) Training and Development Agency for Schools, Results of the Newly Qualified Teacher Survey. Online. https://www.education.gov.uk/publications/RSG/AllRsgPublications/Page11/TDA-NQT-2009 (accessed 16 November 2011).

Wagner, A. (2005) 'Unsettling the academy: Working through the challenges of anti-racist pedagogy'. *Race, Ethnicity and Education,* 8(3), 261–75.

Wilkins, C. and Lall, R. (2010) 'Getting by or getting on? Black student teachers' experiences of teacher education'. *Race Equality Teaching,* 28(2), 19–26.

WRECC (1999) (Wolverhampton Race Equality Council Consortium) *Recruitment and Retention of Teachers from Ethnic Minority Communities.* Wolverhampton: WRECC.

INDEX

undergraduate programmes, links
with 13

Wagner, A. 44
'whiteness' 56
Wilkins, C. 56
withdrawal by students 31–2; *see also*
retention of BME students
workshops: for students, pre-admission
13, 21; for tutors 13, 45–6, 49

.